Media User's Guide

PSYCHOLOGY

SIXTH EDITION

Carole Wade

Carol Tavris

PRENTICE HALL, Upper Saddle River, NJ 07458

Copyright © 2000 by Prentice-Hall, Inc.
Upper Saddle River, New Jersey 07458

Printed in the United States of America

10 9 8 7 6 5 4 3 2 1

ISBN 0-13-018088-2

TRADEMARK INFORMATION:
America Online is a registered trademark of America Online, Inc.;
CompuServe is a registered trademark of CompuServe, Incorporated;
Microsoft Windows is a trademark of Microsoft Corporation;
Mosaic is copyrighted by the Board of Trustees of the University of Illinois (UI);
Netscape Navigator is a registered trademark of Netscape Communications Corporation;
JavaScript is a registered trademark of Sun Microsystems;
Internet Explorer is a registered trademark of Microsoft Corporation.

The authors and publisher of this manual have used their best efforts in preparing this book. The authors and publisher make no warranty of any kind, expressed or implied, with regard to these programs or the documentation contained in this book. The author and publisher shall not be liable in any event for incidental or consequential damages in connection with, or arising out of, the furnishing, performance, or use of the programs described in this book.

Contents

Preface   v

A Unique Online Study Resource: The Companion Website™   1

Guide to The Psychology Place™   21

Psychology on the Internet 1999–2000: A Prentice Hall Guide   59

Preface

This *Media User's Guide* is provided to help you navigate your way through the Psychology Interactive Center website that accompanies ***Psychology***, Sixth Edition, by Carole Wade and Carol Tavris.

The Psychology Interactive Center is divided into two sections:

- **The Companion Website** is a "free" site that allows you to check your comprehension and retention of the content of each chapter of the textbook. It provides review material and graded self-tests that will help you prepare for the actual tests and quizzes given by your instructor.

- **The Psychology Place** is available on a subscription basis only, and subscriptions are provided free of charge to students who purchase new copies of Wade and Tavris's ***Psychology***. The Activation ID and Password that allows you to access your free subscription can be found on the inside front cover of this *Media User's Guide*, which is packaged with all new copies of ***Psychology***.

- Subscriptions expire six months after the initial log-on, so if you bought a used book and a used *Media User's Guide*, chances are that your Activation ID and Password have already expired.

- If you bought a used book and have an expired Activation ID, you may purchase a new subscription by either buying a new textbook OR by ordering a new *Media User's Guide* from your college bookstore.

Organization of This Guide

This guide is divided into three parts:

- *Part One* describes **The Companion Website** and provides navigation tools for using this valuable study aid.

- *Part Two* describes the content of **The Psychology Place**.

- *Part Three* presents a guide to information on the Internet that should be of interest to students of psychology at all levels of the curriculum.

Logging On

First-time users may log on to the *Psychology Interactive Center* through the following URL: http://www.prenhall.com/wade

Once you access this site, you should choose the Sixth Edition of Carole Wade and Carol Tavris's ***Psychology***.

After you click on the Sixth Edition, you'll have a choice of entering the free **Companion Website** area or the subscription-based **Psychology Place** area. If you choose **The Companion Website**, you'll have an opportunity to customize the site by creating a profile for yourself (see Part One). If you choose **The Psychology Place**, you'll be asked to enter the Activation ID and Password that appear on the front cover of this *Media User's Guide*. As part of your initial log-in, you'll have the opportunity to create your own Password. It is recommended that you write your Activation ID and Password down and keep it in a secure place.

Introductory Psychology is a richly rewarding course that you will most likely remember for the rest of your life. Enjoy!

A Unique Online Study Resource

The Companion Website™

1 Locating Companion Websites   3
2 Getting Started   4
3 Navigation   9
4 The Modules   10

A Unique Online Study Resource
The Companion Website™

As a student you are no doubt familiar with the various supplements produced in conjunction with your textbooks. From videotapes to workbooks, these tools are designed to reinforce the core concepts presented by textbook authors. In addition to traditional print study guides, Prentice Hall now offers online study guides called Companion Websites. To date, over 1,000,000 students like you have visited Prentice Hall's text-specific Companion Websites.

Prentice Hall Companion Websites allow you to:

- identify key topics in your course.
- take interactive quizzes.
- receive immediate feedback on your answers.
- send your results to instructors via e-mail.
- search the Internet using links that have been selected by field experts.

Companion Websites are easy to use. Their standardized design leads you carefully from one activity to the next, chapter by chapter. Online study guides not only give you a better understanding of the core concepts presented in your textbooks, but they also focus your attention on the most important material in every chapter. Most of all, Companion Websites help you use your study time more effectively.

Section 1
Locating Companion Websites

Not sure if your book has a Companion Website? Visiting the Prentice Hall Companion Website Gallery is the simplest way to find out. Go to the Prentice Hall website at **http://www.prenhall.com** and click on *Companion Website Gallery* in the upper right-hand corner of the screen. Then, in the empty box on the black navigation bar, enter the last name of your textbook's author. To generate a list of Websites that meet your criteria, click on the *Search* button. For example, a search for "Wade" would yield the screen shown in Figure 1. Select the appropriate book by looking at the covers, hyperlinked titles, and brief descriptions.

Notice that some sites are labeled "demo." As such sites are currently under development, you can access only one or two chapters of sample content. Check back frequently since Prentice Hall is constantly adding new titles to the Companion Website Gallery.

Another way to see whether a particular book has a Companion Website is to type the following URL into your Location Toolbar: **http://www.prenhall.com/(lead author)**. The text in parenthesis should be replaced with the name of the lead author of your Prentice Hall textbook. For example, the address for *Psychology* by Carole Wade and Carol Tavris is **http://www.prenhall.com/wade**.

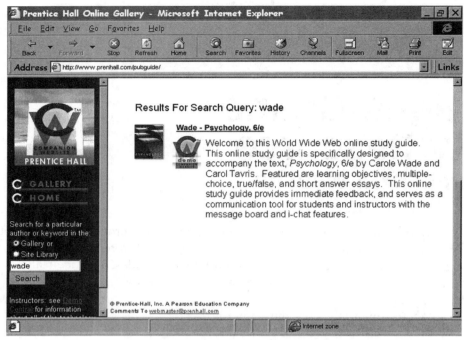

Figure 1. Entering an author's name and clicking on the *Search* button will generate a list of Websites that meet your criteria.

Section 2
Getting Started

On the first page of every Humanities and Social Sciences Companion Website you will find two frames (Figure 2):

Left frame: Navigation Bar

- Syllabus Manager™
- Carol Carter's Student Success Web Supersite
- Your Profile
- Help

Right frame: Content Window

- Link to Web Catalog
- Website Features
- Chapter Menu
- Begin Button

This section will walk you through each of these components.

Navigation Bar

Syllabus Manager

Every Companion Website integrates Syllabus Manager, an online syllabus creation and management utility. After an instructor has created a syllabus using Syllabus Manager, students may enter the syllabus for their course section from any point in the Companion Website. To see whether your instructor has

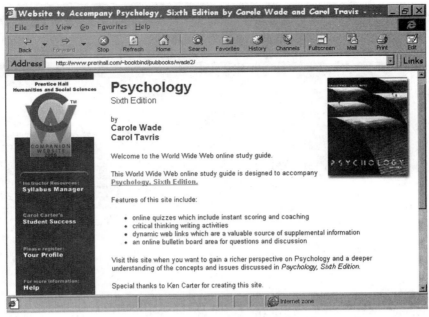

Figure 2. The first page of every Companion Website is divided into two frames: the navigation bar and the content window.

created an online syllabus for your course, click on the *Syllabus Manager* or *Syllabus* button. In the Student Login Window (Figure 3), you have the option of searching by *Instructor's Last Name, Instructor's E-Mail Address,* or *School Name.*

After choosing the button next to your instructor's name, click on the *Search Now* button at the bottom of the screen.

Note that your instructor can create different syllabi for each section he or she teaches; be sure to check the section column (Figure 4) before you click on *Open Syllabus.* If your instructor has password-protected the syllabus, you will need to enter the correct password in the Logon screen (Figure 5) before you can continue. Lost passwords can be requested by using the form at the bottom of the screen.

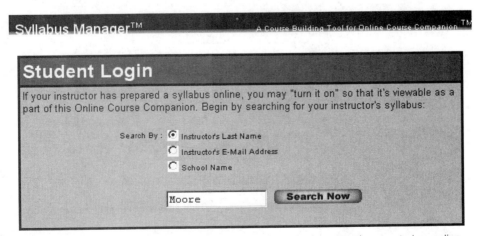

Figure 3. Use the Student Login Window to see whether your instructor has created an online syllabus for your course.

Search Result

	Last, First Name	School Name
○	MCPHAUL-MOORE, ELIZABETH	PIEDMONT COMMUNITY COLLEGE
○	Moore, Chris	Citrus College
○	Moore, Gene	Lake Region High School
●	Moore, Gina	Pearson University
○	moore, Jason	cal st fullerton
○	Moore, John	Tidewater Community College

Figure 4. When the search engine generates a list of several syllabi, make sure you select the syllabus for your section.

After you gain access to the correct syllabus, course summary information appears in the right frame and a calendar appears in the left frame of the Companion Website (Figure 6). Class dates are highlighted in white, and assignment due dates appear in blue. Clicking on a blue date reveals the assignment for that particular day. To save time, the Companion Website activities for each assignment are linked directly from the syllabus to actual content modules.

Use the following directions to print your syllabus:

- Select the syllabus frame by clicking anywhere on the white background of the syllabus.
- Select *File* from top menu bar and then select *Print Frame . . .*
- Make proper printer settings and click *OK*.

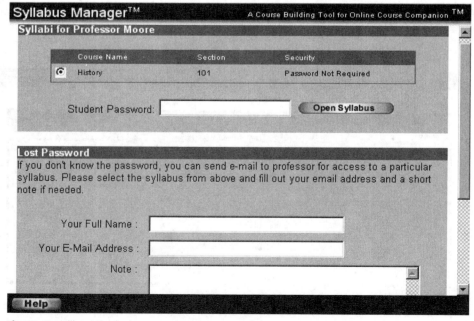

Figure 5. Fill out the login screen to enter your syllabus.

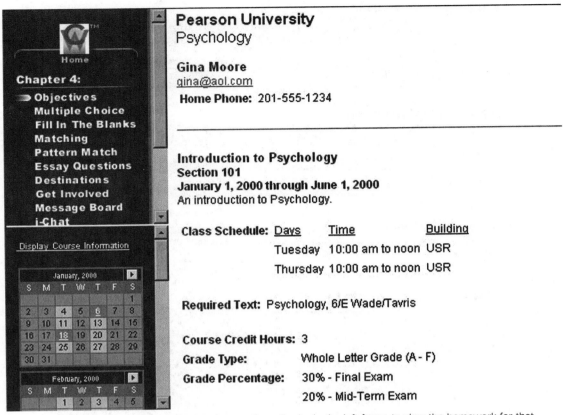

Figure 6. Click on a blue assignment due date on the calendar in the left frame to view the homework for that particular class.

Carol Carter's Student Success Web Supersite

Geared towards high school graduates, college students, returning students, and career changers, this resource site is designed to help students select the appropriate path to meet their educational needs. Features include:

- exploration of different majors.
- answers to study skill questions.
- advice from career counselors.
- brief biographies designed to inspire lifelong learners.
- Web links to interesting sites related to student success.

Your Profile

As mentioned in the overview, Companion Websites not only allow you to take interactive quizzes, but they also give you the opportunity to send your results to an instructor via e-mail. The *Profile* feature lets you standardize the submission of your quiz results. By (carefully) entering your personal information in Figure 7, you can avoid retyping it every time you need to submit homework. Once saved, the information will appear automatically whenever it's required. Remember that you MUST click on the *E-mail Results* button in the *Results Reporter* each time you want to send data to your instructor.

You may return to this screen to modify your profile at any time by clicking the *Profile* button located on the navigation bar throughout the site.

After you enter your personal data, remember to check the all of the appropriate boxes under "Send my quiz results to" (Figure 8). If you and your recipients prefer to receive your results in the body of an e-

Personal Information

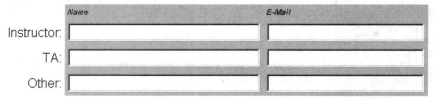

	First	Last
My Name:		

| E-mail: | | |

Instructor Information

	Name	E-Mail
Instructor:		
TA:		
Other:		

Figure 7. This form gives you the opportunity to send your results to an instructor via e-mail. By carefully entering your personal information, you can avoid retyping it every time you need to submit homework.

Send my quiz results to:

☐	Myself:	As plain text ▾
☐	Instructor:	As plain text ▾
☐	TA:	As plain text ▾
☐	Other:	As plain text ▾

Figure 8. By filling out this form you not only select the recipients of your quiz results, but you also select the format of your messages.

mail message, select either "as plain text" or "as HTML" (for *Navigator* or *Internet Explorer* e-mail). On the other hand, if you and your recipients prefer to receive your results as an attachment, select either "as text attachment" or "as HTML attachment" (for *Navigator* or *Internet Explorer* e-mail). Please note that you should always e-mail yourself a copy of your results because Prentice Hall will not save a backup copy.

Due to the volume of submissions, Companion Website e-mail is batched and sent out at thirty minute intervals. Depending on when you send your results to our server for distribution, it may take up to thirty minutes for your results to arrive in your professor's inbox. Keep this in mind when submitting homework assignments.

In the *Profile* area you can also subscribe to the site mailing list by entering your name and e-mail address. Companion Website mailing lists alert users of site updates, i-Chat events, and other items directly related to the textbook or website. Prentice Hall does not use mailing lists for marketing or "spam" e-mail purposes.

Help

This brief overview of Companion Website technology addresses questions that other users have had in the past. Topics are organized by module type in the left-hand navigation bar. To learn more about a particular feature, simply click on its name.

Content Window

In addition to a list of website features, the content window on the first page of every Companion Website contains a link to the Web Catalog. Visit the Web Catalog to read a summary of the textbook and view a complete table of contents. To enter the site, (1) select a chapter from the pull-down menu at the bottom of the screen and (2) click *Begin* (Figure 9).

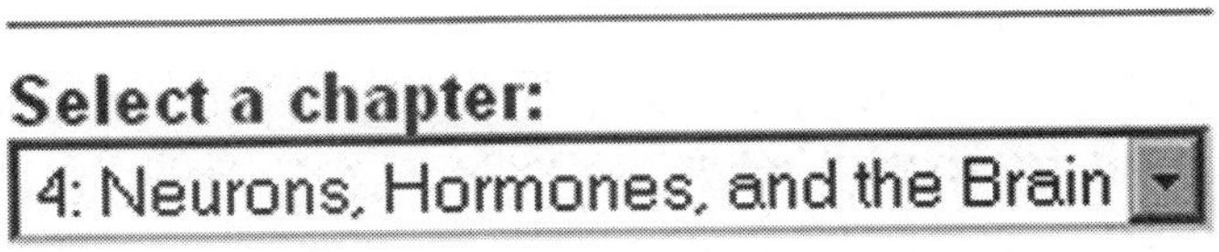

Select a chapter:
4: Neurons, Hormones, and the Brain ▾

Figure 9. To enter a Companion Website, select a chapter from the pull-down menu at the bottom of the screen and click *Begin*.

Section 3
Navigation

In order to move through a Companion Website effectively, you should use the navigation bar in the left frame of the browser window. The top of the navigation bar (Figure 10) offers controls for moving to the previous chapter, the next chapter, or to the top of the site (the index page).

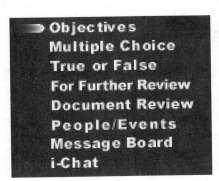

Figure 10. The top of the navigation bar offers controls for moving to the previous chapter, the next chapter, or to the top of the site (the index page).

The middle of the navigation bar (Figure 11) provides links directly to the quiz, research, and communication modules discussed later in this document. Sometimes this area will also include links to individual modules that have been gathered into groups.

Objectives
Multiple Choice
True or False
For Further Review
Document Review
People/Events
Message Board
i-Chat

Figure 11. The middle of the navigation bar provides links directly to the quiz, research, and communication modules.

The bottom portion of the navigation bar (Figure 12) contains links to the Help files, User Profile, Feedback, Site Search, and Course Syllabus, if available.

Other Options:
Help
Your Profile
Feedback
Site Search
→ Syllabus

Figure 12. The bottom portion of the navigation bar contains links to the help files, user profile, feedback, site search, and course syllabus.

Section 4
The Modules

Objectives
The opening page of every chapter defines the unit by providing a summary of the topics covered. This summary can be a list of learning goals for the chapter, a brief introduction/overview of the chapter, or a combination of the two formats.

Multiple Choice
As in traditional learning environments, *Multiple Choice* quizzes are one of the most popular methods of online testing. In fact, the majority of Prentice Hall Companion Websites include at least one *Multiple Choice* quiz. Depending on which book you are using, this quiz module may have a name other than "Multiple Choice." Sample names range from "Review I" to "Elements."

1. [Hint] The peripheral nervous system

○ is made up of the brain and spinal cord.
○ depends exclusively on sensory neurons.
○ depends exclusively on motor neurons.
○ handles the central nervous system's input and output.

Figure 13.   This is an example of a *Multiple Choice* question.

Figure 13 is from an actual *Multiple Choice* quiz module. Each question consists of the following elements:

- the question.
- a *Hint* that will open in a new, smaller browser window.
- the possible answers.

In order to select an answer, mark the circle in front of it with your mouse. When you have completed the quiz, click on the *Submit for Grade* button at the bottom of the page to send your answers to the *Results Reporter* (see page 14).

True or False
True or False quizzes are another popular feature of Companion Websites. Depending on the book you are using, this module may have a name other than "True or False."

1. [Hint] The term "mind" in modern-day psychology refers only to conscious mental states.

○ FALSE
○ TRUE

Figure 14.   This is an example of a True or False question.

Figure 14 is an example from an actual *True or False* quiz module. Each question consists of the following elements:

- the question.
- a *Hint* that will open in a new, smaller browser window.
- the two possible answers.

In order to select an answer, mark the circle in front of it with your mouse. When you have completed the quiz, click on the *Submit for Grade* button at the bottom of the page to send your answers to the *Results Reporter* (see page 14).

Fill in the Blanks

Depending on which book you are using, this quiz module may have a name other than "Fill in the Blanks."

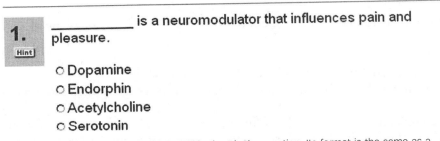

Figure 15. This is an example of a *Fill in the Blanks* question. Its format is the same as a traditional *Multiple Choice* question.

Figure 15 is from an actual *Fill in the Blanks* quiz module. Each question consists of the following elements:

- the question with a blank line.
- a *Hint* that will open in a new, smaller browser window.
- a list of possible answers that could fill in the blank line.

In order to select an answer, mark the circle in front of it with your mouse. When you have completed the quiz, click on the *Submit for Grade* button at the bottom of the page to send your answers to the *Results Reporter* (see page 14).

Essay

Depending on the book you are using, this quiz module may have a name other than Essay. Some examples include "Historical Content" and "Journal Assignment." *Essay* modules may contain a block of introductory text and/or images before the questions.

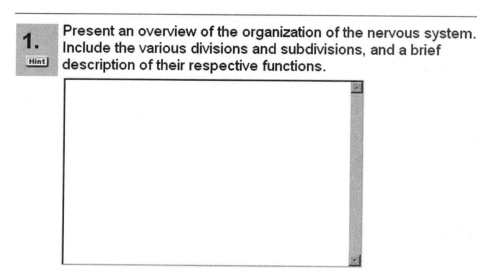

Figure 16. This is an example of an *Essay* question.

Figure 16 is from an actual *Essay* module. Each question consists of the following elements:

- a question.
- an optional *Hint* that will open in a new, smaller browser window.
- a large box, in which you type (or cut-and-paste from another application) your essay.

When you have completed the quiz, click on the *Submit for Grade* button at the bottom of the page to send your answers to the *Results Reporter* (see page 14). Essay questions have to be manually graded by your instructor, but the *Results Reporter* will tell which questions you answered and may give you some general feedback.

Pattern Match

Pattern Match is the newest addition to the Companion Website question library. Although similar in format to traditional *Fill in the Blanks* questions, *Pattern Match* eliminates the list of possible choices, forcing you to generate your own answer. Depending on what book you are using, this quiz module may have a name other than "Pattern Match."

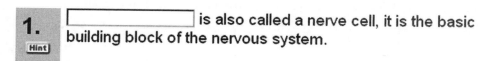

Figure 17. This is an example of a *Pattern Match* question.

Figure 17 is from a *Pattern Match* quiz module. Each question consists of the following elements:

- the question.
- a *Hint* that will open in a new, smaller browser window.
- a text entry box.

To enter an answer, click your cursor within the box and begin typing. When you have completed the quiz, click on the *Submit for Grade* button at the bottom of the page to send your answers to the *Results Reporter* (see page 14).

Labeling

Labeling exercises consist of images with letters that correspond to specific areas. To identify the areas, you select terms from a list of below the image. Depending on which book you are using, this quiz module may have a name other than "Labeling."

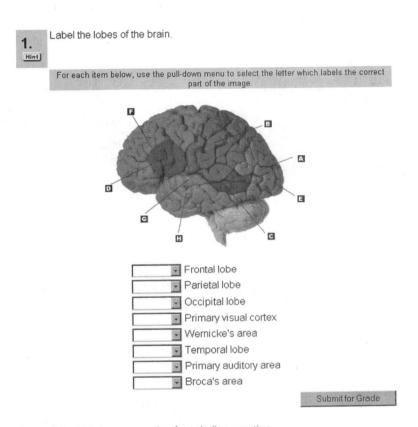

Figure 18. This is an example of a *Labeling* question.

Figure 18 is from a *Labeling* quiz module. To answer the questions:

- Read the introductory text. Click on the *Hint* link if you need some help. *Hints* will open in a new, smaller browser window.
- Examine the image.
- After reading the terms or descriptions, use the pull-down menus to select the letter that corresponds with the text to the right of the menu.

When you have completed the quiz, click on the *Submit for Grade* button at the bottom of the page to send your answers to the *Results Reporter* (see page 14).

Results Reporter

Once you have submitted your work through the *Submit* button, your answers are passed to the automatic grader and your grades are displayed in the *Results Reporter*. This section will explain what each part of the *Results Reporter* displays.

The first part of the *Results Reporter* summarizes how you did, beginning with the percentage of questions you answered correctly (in Figure 19, 70%). You are also shown graphically how many questions you answered correctly and/or incorrectly, as well as the number of questions you didn't answer. Sometimes, the *Results Reporter* will include information about the amount of time you took to complete the quiz. The grading of *Essay* modules cannot be automated so the *Results Reporter* will only display a listing of how many questions you answered.

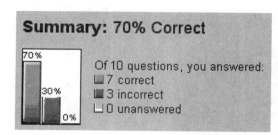

Figure 19. The first part of the *Results Reporter* summarizes how you did, beginning with the percentage of questions you answered correctly. You are also shown graphically how many questions you answered correctly and/or incorrectly, as well as the number of questions you didn't answer.

The bulk of the *Results Reporter* is a question-by-question examination of your responses which looks like this:

1. Incorrect   Marriage forms are similar across social and cultural groups.
Your Answer: TRUE
The correct answer: FALSE

The correct answer is FALSE because marriage forms vary across societal and cultural groups (see p. 2).

The top line shows the question number, whether you got the answer Correct or Incorrect, and the text of the question. Next, the *Results Reporter* lists **Your answer** and **The correct answer**. Finally, depending upon the book you are using, the report may include an explanation of why your answer was correct or incorrect and where to look for additional information in your textbook.

At the bottom of the *Results Reporter* screen you can enter contact information for the people to whom you would like to send your grades (Figure 20). If your recipients prefer to receive your results in the body of an e-mail message, select either "as plain text" or "as HTML" (for Netscape or *Explorer* e-mail). On the other hand, if your recipients prefer to receive your results as an attachment, select either "as text attachment" or "as HTML attachment" (for *Navigator* or *Explorer* e-mail). Please note that you should always e-mail yourself a copy of your results because Prentice Hall will not save a back-up copy.

As discussed earlier, the *Profile* feature lets you standardize the submission of your quiz results. By (carefully) entering your personal information in this screen, you can avoid retyping it every time you need to submit homework. Once saved, the information will appear automatically whenever it's required.

Remember that you MUST click on the *E-mail Results* button at the bottom of the *Results Reporter* each time you want to send results to an instructor.

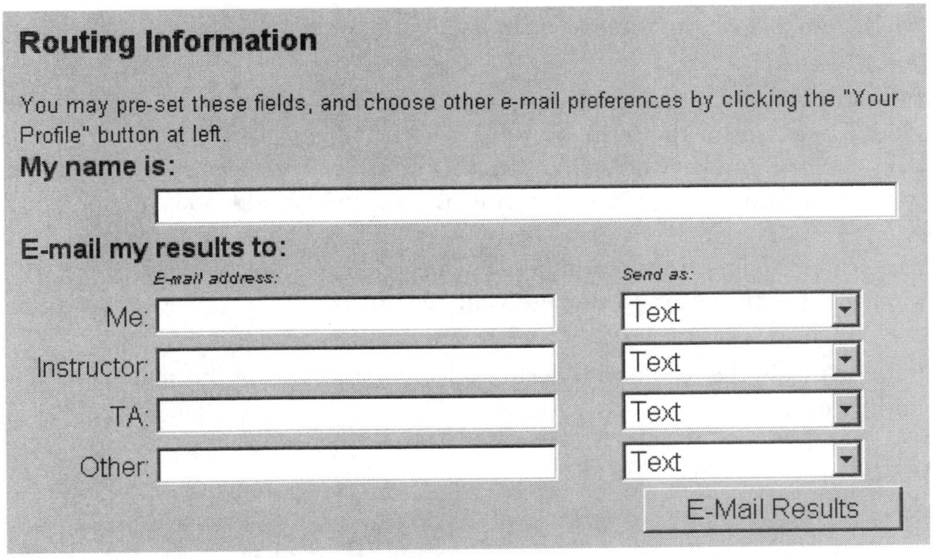

Routing Information

You may pre-set these fields, and choose other e-mail preferences by clicking the "Your Profile" button at left.

My name is:

E-mail my results to:

E-mail address: Send as:

Me: [ ] | Text ▾
Instructor: [ ] | Text ▾
TA: [ ] | Text ▾
Other: [ ] | Text ▾

E-Mail Results

Figure 20. By filling out this form you not only select the recipients of your quiz results, but you also select the format of your messages.

Destinations

This module contains a list of Internet resources relevant to the work in your course. Depending on which book you are using, this module may have a name other than "Destinations." Common titles include "Web Destinations" and "Online Resources."

Each *Destinations* entry will look like this:

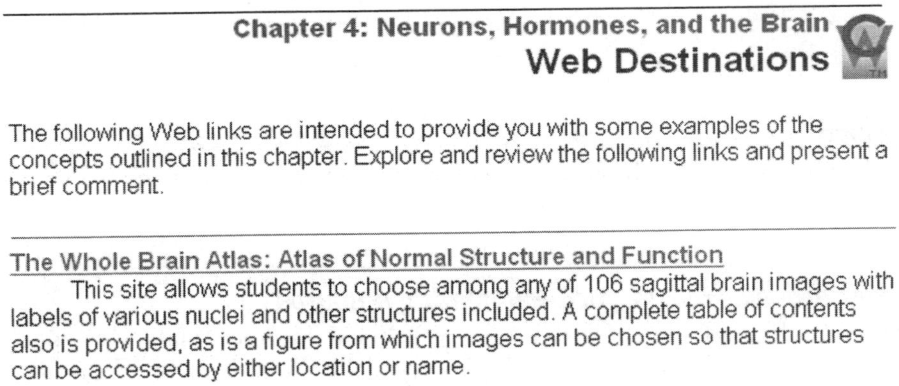

Chapter 4: Neurons, Hormones, and the Brain
Web Destinations

The following Web links are intended to provide you with some examples of the concepts outlined in this chapter. Explore and review the following links and present a brief comment.

The Whole Brain Atlas: Atlas of Normal Structure and Function
This site allows students to choose among any of 106 sagittal brain images with labels of various nuclei and other structures included. A complete table of contents also is provided, as is a figure from which images can be chosen so that structures can be accessed by either location or name.

Please note that these resources generally link to sites outside of Prentice Hall. To visit a particular site, click on the underlined word or phrase (the hypertext link). This link will open a new, smaller browser window containing the information you requested. When finished with the link, return to your Companion Website by closing the smaller window.

Net Search

Net Search allows you to search the Internet based on keywords specified in each Companion Website chapter. Depending on the book you are using, this module may have a name other than "Net Search."

Figure 21 is from a *Net Search* module. To use *Net Search*:

- Read the introductory text, which may include specific instructions or other guidance on how to conduct a search for the terms listed.
- Click on one or more keywords from the list of terms. The term or terms will be added to the empty text box. You can also type in terms of your own or add Boolean operators, such as AND, NOT, OR, +, etc.
- Select a search engine from the pull-down menu.
- Click on the *Search* button to execute your search.

If your search doesn't yield the results you desire, select another one of the search engines from the pull-down menu and try again.

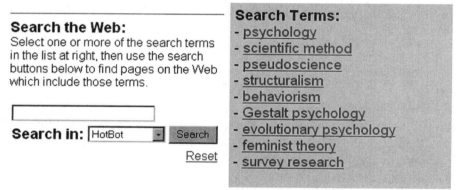

Figure 21. *Net Search* allows you to search the Internet based on keywords specified in each Companion Website chapter.

Message Board

Prentice Hall Message Boards use browser technology to provide students and instructors with a national forum to discuss topics related to their studies.

Configuring Your Browser for Prentice Hall Message Boards

If your system is configured correctly, when you access a Prentice Hall Message Board through a Companion Website, you will already be viewing the virtual bulletin board in your browser. If this is not the case, you are probably configured incorrectly. See the *Online Help* files for instructions on configuring your software.

Reading Messages

Upon entering the message board (Figure 22), you will see a list of messages in the lower portion of the screen. If there are replies to a message, they will be presented in a hierarchy that displays the reply structure. To see this hierarchy, click on the plus side on the *All* button or on the small green arrows next to the subject titles. Groups of related messages are commonly called *threads* of conversation.

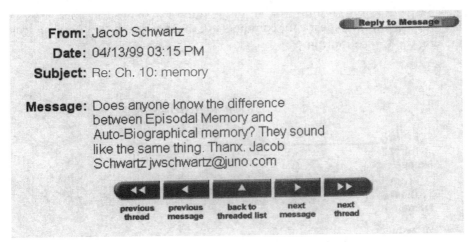

Post New Message

| ← | All | → |

Subject ▼	Sender ▼	Date ▼
No Subject	Doe, Anonymous	12/18/98 01:28 PM
▷2301-090 with prof crane	Doe, Anonymous	01/12/99 06:40 PM
pysc 2301-90 prof crane	kingsbury, lisa	01/22/99 12:15 PM
quiz	Doe, Anonymous	02/07/99 10:58 PM
Class Project	Doe, Anonymous	02/13/99 10:11 PM
No Subject	Doe, Anonymous	02/22/99 01:02 PM
▷Psyc6170-01	Guimaraes, Debora	03/01/99 02:06 PM
▷Downloads	Becker, Catherine	03/02/99 12:02 PM
▷6170	Sexton, Ginna	03/05/99 10:45 AM
6170-01	Baptista, Niosoty	03/09/99 06:27 PM

Figure 22. Upon entering the message board, you will see a list of messages in the lower portion of the screen.

Click on a subject title, and the message will appear in the lower window of the browser above a navigation bar (Figure 23). Use the buttons to read through the messages in a conversation, move to another thread, or return to the main list of postings.

Reply to Message

From: Jacob Schwartz

Date: 04/13/99 03:15 PM

Subject: Re: Ch. 10: memory

Message: Does anyone know the difference between Episodal Memory and Auto-Biographical memory? They sound like the same thing. Thanx. Jacob Schwartz jwschwartz@juno.com

◀◀	◀	▲	▶	▶▶
previous thread	previous message	back to threaded list	next message	next thread

Figure 23. Messages appear in the lower window above a navigation bar.

To post a message, select the *Post New Message* button above the main index of messages (Figure 23). When the form opens in the lower frame (Figure 24), enter your name, subject title, and message in the appropriate fields. When you are finished, click on the *Done – Post Message* button to post your comments to the message board. You can leave this screen at any time by clicking the *Cancel* button.

17

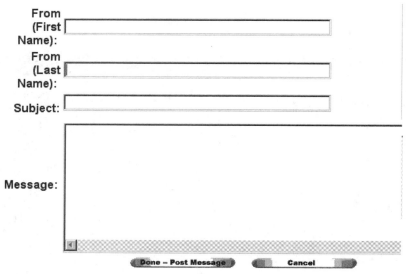

From (First Name):

From (Last Name):

Subject:

Message:

Done – Post Message   Cancel

Figure 24. To post a message to a message board, click on the *Post New Message* button.

To encourage discussion and debate, your reply to an existing message can be associated with an original posting. In order to do this, view the message to which you would like to respond and click on the *Reply to Message* button in the upper left-hand corner of the window (Figure 23). You will be presented with a window similar to the form for creating new messages, but the *Subject* field will be automatically generated (Figure 25). Enter your name and message in the appropriate fields. When you are finished, click on the *Done – Post Message* button to post your comments to the message board. You can leave this screen at any time by clicking the *Cancel* button.

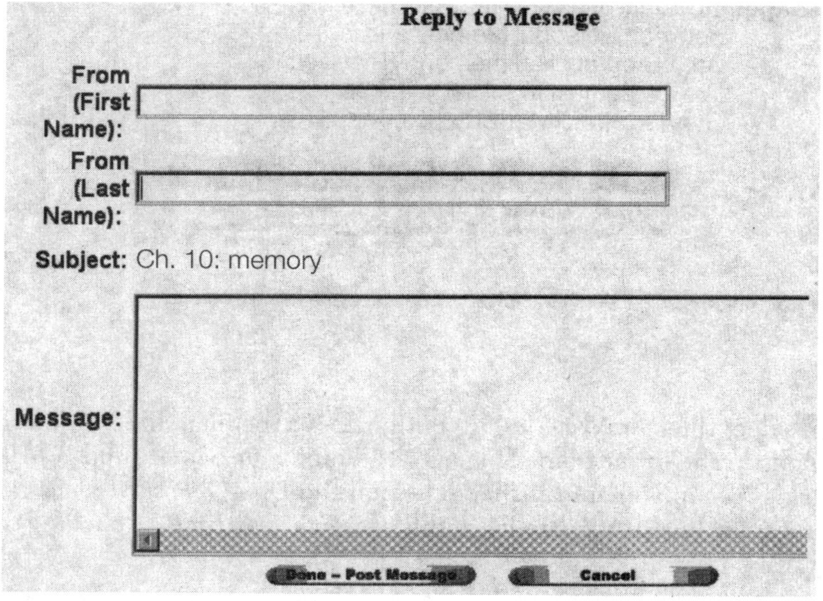

Reply to Message

From (First Name):

From (Last Name):

Subject: Ch. 10: memory

Message:

Done – Post Message   Cancel

Figure 25. When replying to a message, the Subject field will be automatically generated.

i-Chat

I-Chat not only allows instructors to host private class discussions, invite guest speakers to class, and reach students easily, but it also gives you the opportunity to meet students from around the world. In order to gain full functionality of Prentice Hall chat rooms, we recommend that you use the *i-Chat* plug-in. If you choose not to do so, *i-Chat* is also accessible using Java or HTML clients (your browser will automatically select the client that provides the most features).

To enter *i-Chat*:

- Download the *i-Chat* plug-in (accessible from our tune-up page).
- Click on the *i-Chat* button on your Companion Website navigation bar.
- Enter a nickname for yourself.
- Select your chat type. We recommend the default setting.
- Click on the *Enter Chat Area* button.

Although the top region may contain some introductory text or instructions, the bottom region is the actual *i-Chat* client area (Figure 26). Your name and the name of the other users will appear in this area as will the text of the chat. At the bottom of the chat client area, you will find the text entry area. You can begin to participate by simply typing a message into this region and pressing *Enter*.

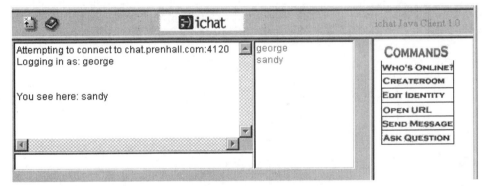

Figure 26. At the bottom of the chat client area, you will find the text entry area. You can begin to participate by simply typing a message into this region and pressing *Enter*.

Once you've mastered the basics of chatting, you may want to experiment with the additional menu choices available. For help when you are in *i-chat*, use the help icon that resembles a book with a question mark.

Advanced i-Chat Features

Sending Private Messages.   Private messages can be sent to individual users through the client menu bar. Click on the icon of the person in silhouette. A new window asking for the recipient and the private message will be generated.

Creating a Private Room for Your Online Study Group.   Private rooms can also be set up for discussions limited to only a few people. One member of the group should create the room using the *Create Private Room* option under the *Commands* sub-menu of the chat menu. Fill out the form requesting a private room. If you have a URL you would like to display in the banner, type it in the URL field; otherwise you can use a default URL such as **http://www.prenhall.com**. In order for others to join you in the room, you have to invite them by using the */invite {username}* command.

The room will be removed when all participants have left. Private rooms can be exited by using the Navigation sub-menu of the chat menu, or by using the */go {exitname}* command.

Groups

Groups can have many names, but their basic premise is to gather several quiz, research, or communication modules into one area, thereby reducing clutter on the navigation bar. Figure 27 is an example of a group that contains several quizzes. Typical groups contain navigation icons and some instructions.

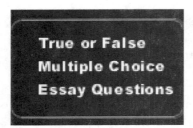

Figure 27. This is an example of a group of modules. Note that the icons work just like the ones in the main navigation bar.

Other Modules

Because technology changes rapidly, you may encounter modules in a Companion Website that are not covered in this book. Most often the URLs for such modules will contain the words "custom.html." As Prentice Hall introduces new technologies to Companion Websites, helpful instructions will be incorporated within the modules as well as within the online *Help* pages. If you can't find an answer to your problems within these pages, please contact Prentice Hall's help support staff via e-mail:

web_tech_support@prenhall.com

To help in answering your questions quickly, please carefully describe your problem(s) and the browser you are using.

Guide to
The Psychology Place™

A wealth of content is available to you in The Psychology Place. To make it easy for you to see what we have, we've provided a Quick Reference section that gives you a bird's-eye view of the categories and articles available for each chapter. This is followed by a lengthier set of annotations so you can see what each article covers.

Learning Activities

The faculty and publisher of *The Psychology Place* are committed to providing rich and varied learning activities that promote inquiry-based learning on the Web. You will find investigative activities that explore core concepts, research, and current topics related to your introductory psychology course. Online labs and experiments allow you to collect and compare data with other students. You will participate in interactive tutorials and exercises that challenge your criticial thinking skills in important, everyday decisions.

Research News

These articles provide psychology's perspective on real-life events and keep you up-to-date on interesting research that is being done all over the world. Explore information related to your course or find materials for research projects. Each Research News article includes print and Web references that can be used for further research.

Op Ed Essays

The Op Ed Essays are written by guest contributors and challenge us with important new information, ideas, or strategies pertinent to introductory psychology. They are interactive as well, and you are invited to join a collegial dialogue about the issues raised by the contributors.

Scientific American Connection

The Scientific American Connection provides a collection of articles from *Scientific American* magazine selected based on their relevance to introductory psychology. These articles are specially reformatted for the Web and include links to our glossary and to additional Web resources.

Ask Dr. Mike

Got a question about psychology? Well, you've come to the right place! After 15 years of teaching introductory psychology, Dr. Mike Atkinson has heard them all and in this space has provided answers to the most frequently-asked questions.

Quick Reference Guide

	Learning Activities	Research News	Op Ed Essays	Ask Dr. Mike
Chapter One **The Science of Psychology**	Analyzing Arguments: Deciding What to Believe Critical Thinking: I Know It's a Good Thing, but What Is It? Caveat Emptor: Evaluating Knowledge Claims		What are the Implications of National Standards for Teaching Psychology? What Questions are on Psychologists' Minds Today? How did Leading Psychologists Find Psychology?	What's the difference between a psychologist and a psychiatrist? I am interested in becoming a psychiatrist and I am wondering about what it takes to accomplish that? My textbook seems to have a LOT of information. How do I know what's important?
Chapter Two **How Psychologists Do Research**		Animal Rights Activists: Changing Views On Animal Research Placebo Effects May Be as Strong as "Real" Drugs	How Can We Promote Academic Honesty?	Who is the most "famous" psychologist?
Chapter Three **Evolution, Genes, and Behavior**		Nature vs. Nurture: Genes Win Again! Cockroach Pheromones Can Cause Social Dominance Evolutionary Change Before Your Eyes Planum Temporale: Brain Structure Behind Language Evolution?		What does all of this physiological stuff have to do with psychology? Young infants seem to show a preference for looking at faces. Could this be due to the fact that faces are the only things they've seen in the delivery room. I've often heard that "opposites attract." Is this true? Are people who are opposite in physical attractiveness likely to get along?

	Learning Activities	Research News	Op Ed Essays	Ask Dr. Mike
Chapter Four **Neurons, Hormones, and the Brain**	Action at the Synapse	Second Languages and the Brain: New Organization for Later Learners One Eye Open: How Sleeping Ducks Avoid Becoming "Sitting Ducks" Sex Alters the Brain	Are We Hostages to Our Brains?	Does the research on "split-brain" patients suggest a basis for the unconscious? Is the left hemisphere conscious, while the right is unconscious? What is the cause of ambidexterity? What if a neuron doesn't have enough "firing power? Brain tumor? What are some of the side effects? And if you have surgery, what are the chances of not having anything wrong with that person? What's the difference between an action potential and a graded potential?
Chapter Five **Body Rhythms and Mental States** **Scientific American Connection**	Investigating Dreams Drug Use, Abuse and Addictions: Focus on Alcohol Tick Tock Goes the Social and Biological Clock	Cigarette Smoking and Genetics: A Not So Unlikely Combination	Are We Chronically Sleep-Deprived?	What is actually measured when someone measures your "arousal level?" What can you tell me about the drug "ecstasy"? Can you practice to have a lucid dream? How? What is an antihistamine and how does it work? What would happen if someone with Parkinson's disease took cocaine? What is THC and how does it work? Is it possible to walk or act out behavior while dreaming? If you dream that you are falling and if you hit the ground, will you die? Can dreams predict the future? How do you explain the fact that sometimes you dream about something and then it happens?

	Learning Activities	Research News	Op Ed Essays	Ask Dr. Mike
				How do you figure out that a particular symbol stands for something else in a dream? We have been talking a lot in class about ESP. What is your opinion on this subject? How would a behaviorist explain the operation of an aphrodisiac?
Chapter Six **Sensation and Perception**	Investigating Depth Perception	Auditory Perceptual Deficits in Language-Impaired Children Seeing with Your Auditory Cortex Brain Area Represents Local Visual Environments How the Brain "Hears" Sign Language		How do you explain those "magic eye" 3D pictures? What do glasses do? What happens when your eye becomes "blood shot?" Are carrots good for your eyesight? Do cartoons appear to move through the autokinetic effect? When older people begin to have problems with their vision, does this have anything to do with damage to the visual cortex?
Chapter Seven **Learning and Conditioning**	Principles of Learning in the Real World	Should Creativity Be Rewarded? Giving Children Rewards: A Right Way and a Wrong Way Songbird Brain Cell Count Predicts Learning Beyond Pavlov's Dogs		If you punish a response (e.g. bar pressing), what happens when you no longer deliver the punishment? What's the difference among desensitization, counterconditioning, and aversive conditioning? In a counterconditioning procedure, can you get a transfer of fear to the positive stimulus rather than the other way around? Can reinforcement be presented "unconsciously?" Can we learn without being aware?

	Learning Activities	Research News	Op Ed Essays	Ask Dr. Mike
				My students have a tough time in distinguishing between negative reinforcement and punishment. What are some good examples of each? In Pavlov's studies, wouldn't he have trouble controlling the dogs as soon as they entered the experimental room? Wouldn't they learn to salivate at the sight and sound of the door?
Chapter Eight **Behavior in Social and Cultural Context**	Exploring the False Consensus Effect Investigating the Evolutionary Perspective: 3 Dads and a Baby Investigating Social Judgments: Expectations, Stereotypes, and the Impressions We're Left With Investigating Gangs and Behavior	Social Control: Good and Bad for Your Health Predicting Our Own Social Behavior Another Explanation for Differences in Intellectual Performance: Stereotype Threat Racism Requires Racial Categorization The Social Consequences of Affirmative Action When "Harmless" Flirtation Hurts A Psychologist Looks at the Death Penalty Are We Sugarcoating Culture? Thinking Critically About the Study of Diversity Juvenile Violence: Why the Mass Murder at Jonesboro, Arkansas? Ingratiation May Be Considered Slimy But It May Have Its Rewards		What about the effects of watching real violence on TV, for example, on the evening news? Are the results the same as with fictional acts of aggression? Is altruism related to religion, e.g., would a more religious person be less susceptible to bystander effects? We recently saw the videotape entitled "Secret of the Wild Child." This was a NOVA special featuring the unique story of the young girl who was found in California in the early 1970s after having endured almost total social isolation. My students and I were curious to know where and how Genie is today. Could you tell us what became of her? Is the unresponsive bystander effect only found in North America? What do people usually say when they are asked why they failed to help at an emergency situation? Is Frosh Week based at least partly on deindividuation?

Psychology	Learning Activities	Research News	Op Ed Essays	Ask Dr. Mike
				Does conformity play any role in jury decisions?
				Why is timing of the requests so important when using the door-in-the-face technique?
				During times of international conflict, does prejudice within a single country decrease?
				Were people obedient in the Milgram study because they somehow believed that the experimenter was "good," and would not let them do something harmful?
				It seems likely that media violence can influence aggression, but why are people "drawn" to media violence? Is this some kind of natural drive?
				Does conformity play any role in jury decisions?
Chapter Nine **Thinking and Intelligence**	Understanding Mental Models Critical Thinking: I Know It's a Good Thing, but What Is It?	The Growing Popularity of "Emotional Intelligence" Another Measure of Intelligence: Working Memory Numerical Ability In Chimpanzees		What is the "Chitterling Test?" What causes dyslexia? What is savant syndrome and what causes it? If Savants are so good at counting, why can't they make change for $1.00? Can your IQ level change over time? Is the term "mentally retarded" still acceptable? Is it possible to have a mild case of Savant Syndrome? Could this be what "gifted" really means? What is the longest word in the English language?

	Learning Activities	Research News	Op Ed Essays	Ask Dr. Mike
Chapter Ten **Memory** **Scientific American Connection**	Product Claims: Too Good to be True? Test Your Memory	Another Measure of Intelligence: Working Memory	Recovered-memory Experiences: Explaining True and False Delayed Memories of Childhood Sexual Abuse	If the proper cue could be found, would it be possible to retrieve any memory? Is any particular type of music related to memory recall in positive or negative ways? How and why? Can the environmental context influence memory?
Chapter Eleven **Emotion**		Emotion, Memory and the Brain Is Embarrassment a Distinct Emotion?		Are facial expressions reflexive? When I get angry, why does my chest start to hurt? What is a "lie detector?"
Chapter Twelve **Motivation**		Scent of a Woman: The Scientific Sequel	Who or What is to Blame for the Littleton Massacre?	Did TV violence cause the Littleton situation? Do animals imitate? If so, what does this mean?
Chapter Thirteen **Theories of Personality** **Scientific American Connection**	Investigating Graphology: Is the Writing on the Wall?		Challenging the Nurture Assumption	Can a personality test ever be "wrong"? What does Freud have to say about the development of homosexuality in men? What are inkblots made out of and how are they made? In the Freudian structure of the mind, is it fair to say that the Id is "selfish," and that the superego is "good?
Chapter Fourteen **Development Over the Life Span** **Scientific American Connection**		All in Your Head? Attention Disorder May Be Genetic Fear of Death: Our Final Developmental Crisis Primate Caretakers Live Longer Babies, Phonetics, and Mastering Language	Challenging the Nurture Assumption The Power of Parents	What is a "critical period?" Is "Motherese" universal – does this appear in all cultures? Do young children have a conscience? What are the causes of various attachment styles? Is it the parent's behavior or the child's?

	Learning Activities	Research News	Op Ed Essays	Ask Dr. Mike
		Daycare: What's a Parent to Do? Dyslexia Predicted by Decreased Brain Activity Birth Month Predicts Height? Prenatal Experience: More is Not Better Should Parents Intervene in Children's Fights? Even Light Maternal Drinking Affects the Unborn Child Infant Attachment, Adult Curiosity, and Cognitive Closure Childhood Attachment Style: How Stable Over the Life Span?		If eye color is the result of a dominant (brown) allele and a recessive (blue) allele, how can you have green eyes? Using a Mendel table, the color should be either brown or blue, shouldn't it? If a mother smokes during pregnancy, are there any effects on the fetus? To what extent does the lack of infant attachment adversely influence adult behavior? If attachment is strong and secure at an early age, what happens when you move out on your own? Do you have to replace this secure attachment? We recently saw the videotape entitled "Secret of the Wild Child." This was a NOVA special featuring the unique story of the young girl who was found in California in the early 1970s after having endured almost total social isolation. My students and I were curious to know where and how Genie is today. Could you tell us what became of her?
Chapter Fifteen **Health, Stress, and Coping** Scientific American Connection	Drug Use, Abuse and Addictions: Focus on Alcohol	Social Control: Good and Bad for Your Health Regrets? . . . I've Had a Few: Women's Midlife Review and Well-Being Better Living Through Mindfulness Rethinking the Power of Positive Thinking	The Social Usefulness of Self-Esteem: A Skeptical View Building a Positive Social Science for the 21st Century	Does stress help us to remember information (like phone numbers) or does it make us forget? Can meditation heal? I read an article recently where they said that having a "wet dream" was a normal experience and did not reflect a psychological disorder. Is this true or does it really reflect a disorder?

	Learning Activities	Research News	Op Ed Essays	Ask Dr. Mike
		Anger Sensitivity: A Hidden Cost of Child Abuse		
		Classes, Computers, Exams . . . and Beer: College Drinking		
		Coping After Abortion		
		Procrastination May be Dangerous to Your Health and Performance		
		Getting Old: Better Than You Expect		
		Maternal Grooming: A Lifelong Aid to Stress Reduction?		
		Cigarette Smoking and Genetics: A Not So Unlikely Combination		
Chapter Sixteen **Psychological Disorders** **Scientific American Connection**	Investigating Sex Differences in Depression Recognizing Mood Disorders	Teen Suicide—Symptom of a Changing World or Exaggerated Suggestibility in Adolescence Editor's Note: Unabomber Update The Insanity Defense and the Unabomber Trial The Manic-Depressive Brain DSM-IV: How Many Entries for The Book of Names? Manic-Depressive Illness and Creativity Schizophrenic Disorder: When People Hear Voices, Who's Talking? Eating Disorders and Sudden Death Mental Illness: Dangers, Treatment, and Civil Liberties The Social Consequences of Affirmative Action	Who or What is to Blame for the Littleton Massacre?	What is antisocial personality disorder? Can this explain the Littleton shootings? What is an "anxiety attack?" What is bi-polar disease, and how do you get it? What are some symptoms, and is there a cure? Can psychological blindness correct itself? What is the underlying cause of a phobia? What is Tourettes Syndrome? I have a history of bipolar disorder in my family. How can I tell the difference between everyday mood swings and real disorder? Is catharsis a good thing or a bad thing? I've heard both. What is "normal," anyway? If reality is based on perception, how can we label a schizophrenic as "abnormal?"

	Learning Activities	Research News	Op Ed Essays	Ask Dr. Mike
				Is it typical to feel "down" after reading or talking about depression?
				What is the likelihood that the genes for a mental disorder can be passed down from your parents? Would the home environment have any effect?
				Is it considered abnormal to sometimes have feelings of depression and consider suicide?
				With Multiple Personality Disorder, can one of the personalities be ill while the other is healthy?
				Concerning Tourette's Syndrome, does a person have inappropriate behaviors other than swearing, such as inappropriate sexual behavior in public?
				Is Anorexia Nervosa really a form of Anxiety Disorder?
				What is Luvox?
Chapter Seventeen **Approaches to Treatment and Therapy**		Feeling Low This Winter? "A Sunny Disposition" May Help Childhood and Adolescent Depression—To Medicate or Not?		Is electroconvulsive therapy (ECT) always beneficial? I've heard that Prozac has few, if any, side effects. Is this true? Is it common to mix treatments for various disorders, for example, electroconvulsive therapy (ECT) and lithium? I am reading this book about a famous psychiatrist who sexually abused his patient under the influence of amytal. Have you ever heard of this case? What is amytal and what is it used for? What are the effects of long-term use?

Chapter One
The Science of Psychology

 ## Learning Activities

Analyzing Arguments: Deciding What to Believe
Test your critical thinking skills in this activity by Diane Halpern. Analyze persuasive appeals, learn how to identify good reasons and conclusions, and practice the art of analyzing arguments.

Critical Thinking: I Know It's a Good Thing, but What Is It?
This tutorial will help you to review the processes of critical thinking. Examine a few scenarios and test your ability to recognize critical thinking in action.

Caveat Emptor: Evaluating Knowledge Claims
Explore how you can become a good consumer of information. Learn how to evaluate the critical features of knowledge claims that you see in advertising or on the Internet.

 ## Op Ed Essays

What are the Implications of National Standards for Teaching Psychology
By Kenneth A. Weaver, Emporia State University
The author identifies some of the issues and potential pitfalls of setting national standards for teaching high school psychology and invites you to post your views on the issue in the forum.

What Questions are on Psychologists' Minds Today?
by David G Myers, Hope College
What questions are currently driving psychology's most fertile minds? We asked the most oft-cited psychologists in introductory psychology texts and the APA Distinguished Scientific Contribution Award winners from the last decade to tell us, "What is the question you are asking yourself—the question that most fascinates you right now?" Here are their answers.

How did Leading Psychologists Find Psychology?
by David G Myers, Hope College
Why did some of today's leading psychologists enter the field of psychology? We asked the most-often cited psychologists in introductory psychology texts and APA Distinguished Scientific Contribution Award winners from the last decade to tell us their stories. Read the personal narratives of Phil Zimbardo, Elizabeth Loftus, Eliot Aronson— to name just a few.

Ask Dr. Mike

- What's the difference between a psychologist and a psychiatrist?
- I am interested in becoming a psychiatrist and I am wondering about what it takes to accomplish that?
- My textbook seems to have a LOT of information. How do I know what's important?

Chapter Two
How Psychologists Do Research

Research News

Animal Rights Activists: Changing Views On Animal Research

A newly published survey and analysis shows that animal rights activists have shifted some of their views over the past decade. A 1990 survey by psychologist Scott Plous of Wesleyan University revealed that the activists' primary concern was the use of animals in research. A 1996 survey by Plous now shows that while activists still view research animals as an important issue, they have become more concerned about animal agriculture. The newer survey also indicates that activists may be more willing now to discuss their concerns directly with animal researchers instead of engaging in extreme tactics.

Placebo Effects May Be as Strong as "Real" Drugs

Can you be cured by the placebo effect? Reports from several sources suggest that using placebo drugs—substances that have no active ingredients, but which the person believes to have curative power—produces behavioral and physical effects that are about as strong as those produced by "real" drugs. One study claims that placebo effects account for as much as 50 percent of improvement in depressed patients. The power of the placebo effect in therapy has produced a conscientious debate.

Op Ed Essays

How Can We Promote Academic Honesty?
by G. William (Bill) Hill, IV of Kennesaw State University and Stephen F. Davis of Emporia State University

How widespread is cheating? Who cheats, and why? How can we encourage academic integrity? William Hill IV (Kennesaw State) and Stephen F. Davis (Emporia State) put these questions on the table and offer some initial thoughts.

Ask Dr. Mike

- Who is the most "famous" psychologist?

Chapter Three
Evolution, Genes, and Behavior

 Research News

Nature vs. Nurture: Genes Win Again!
One of the longest running debates in psychology is the so-called "nature versus nurture" controversy: Is heredity or environment the primary determinant of human potential?

Cockroach Pheromones Can Cause Social Dominance
The male lobster cockroach has a secret chemical weapon—a pheromone that attracts females and allows them to tell one male from the next. New experiments reveal that variations in the levels of these chemicals actually cause (rather than simply reflect) a male's dominance status in bouts of male-male competition. Additional studies show that a male's environment helps determine the chemical make-up of his alluring odor. This is a striking example of how environmental factors can affect an organism's physiology, and how the physical functioning, in turn, can influence an animal's social behavior.

Evolutionary Change Before Your Eyes
Lizards that were introduced to new habitats containing shorter, thinner vegetation than that found at their original home evolved shorter hind limbs within 10 years. This study is a remarkable demonstration of the speed and extent of the effects of natural selection under conditions requiring adaptation to dramatic environmental change.

Planum Temporale: Brain Structure Behind Language Evolution?
The planum temporale (PT) region of the human brain is associated with language. This area is the brain's most lateralized anatomical structure, meaning that it is much larger in the left hemisphere than in the right. Until now, anatomists believed that humans were unique with regard to this region's asymmetry. However, a recent study reveals that our closest nonhuman relative, the chimpanzee, also shares asymmetry of the planum temporale. Although researchers don't yet know the function of PT asymmetry in the chimpanzee, this anatomical discovery provides new hypotheses regarding the evolution of human language.

 Ask Dr. Mike

- What does all of this physiological stuff have to do with psychology?
- Young infants seem to show a preference for looking at faces. Could this be due to the fact that faces are the only things they've seen in the delivery room.
- I've often heard that "opposites attract." Is this true? Are people who are opposite in physical attractiveness likely to get along?

Chapter Four
Neurons, Hormones, and the Brain

 ### Learning Activities

Action at the Synapse
The synapse is where it's at, if you're a neuron communicating with other neurons in the brain. This highly animated four-part activity focuses on the action at the synapse and some behavioral effects of what happens at the synapse. It includes some review of the action potential, but the emphasis here is on synaptic communication, neurotransmitter effects, and drug effects.

 ### Research News

Second Languages and the Brain: New Organization for Later Learners
Adults who learned two languages during early childhood have a brain organization that differs significantly from those who learned a second language during adolescence. A recent study by a brain-imaging team in New York provides the first direct evidence that in bilingual people, the age at which a second language is acquired influences the physical development of a major language center in the brain.

One Eye Open: How Sleeping Ducks Avoid Becoming "Sitting Ducks"
Nonhuman organisms rely on natural strategies to protect themselves from predators. Recently, researchers discovered a remarkable strategy used by mallard ducks: By sleeping with one eye open and one eye shut, they can keep one brain hemisphere in a sleep state and the other awake and alert for danger. This discovery has some interesting implications for the relationship between brain and behavior.

Sex Alters the Brain
We know that the brain powerfully shapes our behavior, but can behavior also affect the anatomy of the brain? For some time, researchers have known that experience alters brain structure, but now a California neuroscientist has found evidence that engaging in a particular form of behavior can greatly alter the anatomy of individual neurons. Specifically, male rats that engaged in copulatory behavior experience a shrinking in the size of neurons in a specific brain area. These findings may have important implications for the study of human sexuality.

 ### Op Ed Essays

Are We Hostages to Our Brains?
   by Charles W. Perdue, West Virginia State College and James L. Hilton, University of Michigan
Explore this timely and provocative view of the mind-brain relationship. Can we truly distinguish between the brain and mind? Can changing your behavior really change your brain? Professors Perdue and Hilton ask you to examine relevant research and post your perspective in the forum.

Ask Dr. Mike

- Does the research on "split-brain" patients suggest a basis for the unconscious? Is the left hemisphere conscious, while the right is unconscious?
- What is the cause of ambidexterity?
- What if a neuron doesn't have enough "firing power?"
- Brain tumor? What are some of the side effects? And if you have surgery, what are the chances of not having anything wrong with that person?
- What's the difference between an action potential and a graded potential?

Chapter Five
Body Rhythms and Mental States

Learning Activities

Investigating Dreams
Ever wonder about your crazy dreams? Would interpreting your dreams provide you with any special insights? Here's an opportunity to try it yourself and find out. First, review the prevalent dream theories, then, over a three-week period, record and interpret your own dreams. All the materials you'll need are provided here.

Drug Use, Abuse and Addictions: Focus on Alcohol
In this activity, you will examine where drug abuse and addictions begin with a special focus on alcohol and its use among young people today. You will engage in a debate on lowering the drinking age and keep track of your own substance use.

Tick Tock Goes the Social and Biological Clock
Our bodies pull us in some ways; our cultures pull us in others. What are the relative effects of each, how do they interact, how are they changing? Play the Longevity Game and find out how your calculated life expectancy affects your social clock.

Research News

Cigarette Smoking and Genetics: A Not So Unlikely Combination
Why is it easy for some people to quit smoking, while others can't seem to kick the habit? Why do some people start smoking in the first place? New research suggests that part of the answer to these questions may lie in the presence or absence of specific genes. More information about genes identified with smoking risk can ultimately identify who is at risk for nicotine dependence and can help determine the best way to quit smoking.

 **Op Ed Essays**

Are We Chronically Sleep-Deprived?
    by Stanley Coren,
We have heard it, taught it, believed it: We have widely varying sleep needs. We can adapt to less sleep and still function well. In any case, 7 hours is plenty for the average adult.

We have heard, taught, and believed wrongly, argues University of British Columbia neuropsychologist Stanley Coren in his fascinating book *Sleep Thieves* (Free Press, 1996). Evidence ranging from unrestricted sleep length to Canadian traffic accident rates on the day following "Spring forward" drives him to a surprising conclusion: We are biologically prepared for more sleep than we're getting.

 **Scientific American Connection**

The Meaning of Dreams
    by Jonathan Winson (1998)
What are we to make of all our bizarre dreams? Are they merely our brain's best attempt to make sense of random neural firing, as physiological theories have proposed? Or was Freud right that dreams are the "royal road to our unconscious"? Researcher Jonathan Winson has deftly combined elements of those and other theories with his own work to create a clearer explanation of the meaning of our dreams. (See related activity)

 Ask Dr. Mike

- What is actually measured when someone measures your "arousal level"?
- What can you tell me about the drug "ecstasy"?
- Can you practice to have a lucid dream? How?
- What is an antihistamine and how does it work?
- What would happen if someone with Parkinson's disease took cocaine?
- What is THC and how does it work?
- Is it possible to walk or act out behavior while dreaming?
- If you dream that you are falling and if you hit the ground, will you die?
- Can dreams predict the future? How do you explain the fact that sometimes you dream about something and then it happens?
- How do you figure out that a particular symbol stands for something else in a dream?
- We have been talking a lot in class about ESP. What is your opinion on this subject?
- How would a behaviorist explain the operation of an aphrodisiac?

Chapter Six
Sensation and Perception

Learning Activities

Investigating Depth Perception

When looking at a painting, why do we perceive some parts of it as farther away than others? The eye's retina, like a painting or a photograph, is two-dimensional, so how do we perceive the world in three dimensions? In this Activity, you will explore how the brain interprets different depth cues in order to accurately perceive the three-dimensional world. Test your own accuracy in perceiving the depth of objects, and compare your responses with those of fellow students.

Research News

Auditory Perceptual Deficits in Language-Impaired Children

Children affected with Specific Language Impairment (SLI) have severe language deficits but otherwise are intellectually normal. Psychophysical experiments now reveal that SLI children differ from normal children in the way they detect speechlike sounds. This altered form of auditory perception may play a role in the altered form of speech production characteristic of SLI children.

Seeing with Your Auditory Cortex

Modern brain imaging techniques reveal that areas of the human cortex typically activated during auditory speech perception are also activated during the visual component of auditory communications—lip reading. This is of particular interest because lip reading can greatly affect one's ability to perceive speech accurately.

Brain Area Represents Local Visual Environments

Researchers have identified a small portion of the human brain called the "parahippocampal place area" (PPA)—a region that becomes selectively active when we view a local environmental space, such as a room. Through an intriguing series of experiments, researchers demonstrated how the PPA is involved in visual perception by rearranging objects and components of local visual environments. They think the PPA may encode visual memories of the settings we encounter and thereby assist our ability to navigate in local environments.

How the Brain "Hears" Sign Language

How does the brain function when a person is denied input from a major sensory modality? What if that input happens to be spoken language, and what if speech is replaced by a different form of language in an entirely different sensory modality, namely vision? A new study shows that certain areas of the brain that typically respond to spoken language are activated in congenitally deaf people who communicate with sign language. Thus, the language area of the brain functions regardless of whether language is in the form of auditory speech or visual signals.

Ask Dr. Mike

- How do you explain those "magic eye" 3D pictures?
- What do glasses do?
- What happens when your eye becomes "blood shot?"
- Are carrots good for your eyesight?
- Do cartoons appear to move through the autokinetic effect?
- When older people begin to have problems with their vision, does this have anything to do with damage to the visual cortex?

Chapter Seven
Learning and Conditioning

Learning Activities

Principles of Learning in the Real World

What do salivating dogs, pecking pigeons, and bar-pressing rats have to do with real life? In this activity, you will see the key processes in classical conditioning, operant conditioning, and observational learning in action. By interacting with our dog, Buster and our rat, Dexter, you experience the development of a conditioned response and the paradigms for reinforcement and punishment.

Research News

Should Creativity Be Rewarded?

Both folk wisdom and past psychological studies warn parents and educators to avoid the dangers of overusing rewards. Observers, from the casual to the scientific, have suggested that rewarding creativity on a task reduces intrinsic interest and further creativity on that and future tasks. A theory put forth by Robert Eisenberger of the University of Delaware, however, and a new study by he and two colleagues suggests a very different point of view.

Giving Children Rewards: A Right Way and a Wrong Way

Using prizes, such as stars or money, to reward academic effort may not necessarily be as bad as some critics suggest. Indeed, recent research suggests that misuse of rewards may be responsible for the reduction in children's creativity and intrinsic motivation observed in earlier studies. Verbal praise given for effort, rather than for ability, is suggested as the best motivator.

Songbird Brain Cell Count Predicts Learning

Do the numbers of neurons in certain areas of your brain limit how much you are capable of learning? The answer appears to be "yes"—as long as you're a zebra finch. Researchers have found a strong relationship between the number of neurons in one song-production nucleus of the zebra finch brain and the number of song syllables the birds actually learned from social tutors. The neural numbers did not, however, relate to the entire repertoire of all zebra finch songs. This represents a remarkably specific relationship between neuron number and learning rather than instinctive song production in general.

Beyond Pavlov's Dogs
Pavlov's principles of conditioning apply to more than salivating dogs. Recent studies by three research groups demonstrates the importance of Pavlovian conditioning in a wide range of behaviors, such as defense, mating and reproduction, immune system suppression, drug tolerance and addiction.

 Ask Dr. Mike

- If you punish a response (e.g. bar pressing), what happens when you no longer deliver the punishment?
- What's the difference among desensitization, counterconditioning, and aversive conditioning?
- In a counterconditioning procedure, can you get a transfer of fear to the positive stimulus rather than the other way around?
- Can reinforcement be presented "unconsciously?" Can we learn without being aware?
- My students have a tough time in distinguishing between negative reinforcement and punishment. What are some good examples of each?
- In Pavlov's studies, wouldn't he have trouble controlling the dogs as soon as they entered the experimental room? Wouldn't they learn to salivate at the sight and sound of the door?

Chapter Eight
Behavior in Social and Cultural Context

 **Learning Activities**

Exploring the False Consensus Effect
In this activity you will explore how our attitudes shape our behavior. You will take an Opinion Survey and compare your responses to other participants in *The Psychology Place* and a national survey.

Investigating the Evolutionary Perspective: 3 Dads and a Baby
Join us as a participant in this fascinating exploration of the evolutionary perspective on babies' resemblance to their parents. Is he/she a chip off the old block?

**Investigating Social Judgments: Expectations, Stereotypes, and the Impressions
     We're Left With**
In this interactive activity, you discover how stereotypes influence our impressions of others. You will participate in actual research related to social and cognitive psychology. An assessment exercise is included to see your own results.

Investigating Gangs and Behavior
What are gangs? What motivates adolescents to join them? And how can we discourage gang membership? Learn the answers to these questions and discover why social and developmental psychologists are

interested in this phenomenon. Through various activities, you will explore statistics, propose prevention to parents, and design an ideal program to discourage gang involvement.

 Research News

Social Control: Good and Bad for Your Health
Changing a bad habit is never easy. Friends and family may urge you to adopt healthy behaviors, such as exercising regularly, or giving up smoking; but does their urging, no matter how well-intentioned, really help? A new study of "social control" has uncovered some answers that should make loved ones reconsider their efforts.

Predicting Our Own Social Behavior
New research by Janet Swim and Lauri Hyers reminds us again why we need social psychological research - to discover not just how people think they will act, but how (and why) they do act as they do.

Another Explanation for Differences in Intellectual Performance: Stereotype Threat
Claude Steele (1997) suggests that negative stereotypes about women and African-Americans may impair their performance in the classroom and on standardized tests. Steele also suggests that stereotype threat may be responsible for underperformance in the classroom by students from these same two groups. Additionally, he suggests that stereotyped groups may use disidentification, which serves to protect their self-esteem.

Racism Requires Racial Categorization
Social identity theory predicts that people who strongly identify with an in-group will maintain clear boundaries with relevant out-groups. Psychologist Jim Blascovich and his colleagues predicted, and found, that prejudiced people take more time to carefully categorize people whose race is ambiguous.

The Social Consequences of Affirmative Action
Affirmative action programs have created important opportunities for individuals who experience societal discrimination and disadvantage. Such programs are controversial, however, and some have suggested that those who benefit from affirmative action also pay a price in terms of unfavorable attitudes about their capabilities. A new study by two social psychologists from Canada and Wales supports this: They examined public attitudes about a new, relatively unfamiliar, immigrant group, Surinamers, before and after exposure to a media campaign. The information they disseminated was always positive but sometimes included a mention of the group's eligibility for affirmative action. Their results show that the existence of affirmative action affects attitudes towards both the groups and specific individuals who would benefit from such programs.

When "Harmless" Flirtation Hurts
When does a college flirtation cease being harmless fun and start causing damage? It's when your professor is doing the flirting, say psychologists Arthur Satterfield and Charlene Muehlenhard. In two new studies, they examine the effects of an authority figure's flirtatious behavior on college women and how these students then see their own creative performance. The work explores a "gray area" of sexual harassment, and demonstrates how minor flirtation can shake a woman's self-confidence and sense of achievement.

A Psychologist Looks at the Death Penalty
by Mark Costanzo, Claremont McKenna College
Did Karla Faye Tucker's recent execution in Texas serve any constructive purpose? Surveys show that many Americans, virtually alone among people across the industrialized world, believe capital punish-

ment does serve a purpose. Are they right? Mark Costanzo, Chair of the Claremont McKenna College psychology department, has written many articles about capital punishment and has just published a provocative and well-argued book, *Just Revenge: Costs and Consequences of the Death Penalty* (St. Martins Press). Here he gives us a sneak preview of what research shows. Does his evidence and reasoning persuade you that capital punishment just doesn't work? (Mark's book also engages other issues, such as does capital punishment save money? Is it moral? Do Americans support the death penalty?)

Are We Sugarcoating Culture? Thinking Critically About the Study of Diversity by Carole Wade, Dominican College of San Rafael

"Of course I dislike the Nazis," students have recently been heard to say, "but who is to say they were morally wrong? That was a different time and culture." Similarly, in our age of postmodernism and extreme relativism, some students allow respect for cultural diversity to invalidate judgments regarding ethnic cleansing, genital mutilation, and even slavery and human sacrifice. Their expressed nonjudgmentalism provokes Carole Wade, in this crisp and lucid essay, to wonder: Must multiculturalism neutralize moral judgment?

Juvenile Violence: Why the Mass Murder at Jonesboro, Arkansas?

Following the recent mass murder in Jonesboro, Arkansas, involving alleged assailants just 11 and 13 years old, the media and general public posed many questions concerning juvenile violence. A recent article in *American Psychologist* explores these complex questions and summarizes five major misconceptions and controversies surrounding violence in youngsters.

Ingratiation May Be Considered Slimy But It May Have Its Rewards

People who are nice to superiors but difficult with subordinates are often perceived as "slimy" by others, according to recent research. In addition, research suggests that although people who ingratiate themselves with their bosses are disliked by others, these slimy people have a slight edge in being advanced professionally than those who don't.

 Ask Dr. Mike

- What about the effects of watching real violence on TV, for example, on the evening news? Are the results the same as with fictional acts of aggression?
- Is altruism related to religion, e.g., would a more religious person be less susceptible to bystander effects?
- We recently saw the videotape entitled "Secret of the Wild Child." This was a NOVA special featuring the unique story of the young girl who was found in California in the early 1970s after having endured almost total social isolation. My students and I were curious to know where and how Genie is today. Could you tell us what became of her?
- Is the unresponsive bystander effect only found in North America?
- What do people usually say when they are asked why they failed to help at an emergency situation?
- Is Frosh Week based at least partly on deindividuation?
- Does conformity play any role in jury decisions?
- Why is timing of the requests so important when using the door-in-the-face technique?
- During times of international conflict, does prejudice within a single country decrease?
- Were people obedient in the Milgram study because they somehow believed that the experimenter was "good," and would not let them do something harmful?
- It seems likely that media violence can influence aggression, but why are people "drawn" to media violence? Is this some kind of natural drive?
- Does conformity play any role in jury decisions?

Chapter Nine
Thinking and Intelligence

Learning Activities

Understanding Mental Models

Why are there 24 hours in a day? Is broccoli or a chocolate bar healthier food? The answers you give to these questions depend on how you process abstract concepts. Discover how faulty mental processing or mental models work by participating in interactive demonstrations.

Critical Thinking: I Know It's a Good Thing, but What Is It?

This tutorial will help you to review the processes of critical thinking. Examine a few scenarios and test your ability to recognize critical thinking in action.

Research News

The Growing Popularity of "Emotional Intelligence"

The release of Daniel Goleman's best-selling book Emotional Intelligence was one of the top publishing events of 1995, and garnered a giant following for Goleman's argument that emotional intelligence (EQ) can matter more than IQ. Since then, the subject has inspired numerous articles in popular magazines as well as a plethora of web sites. When it comes to those spin-offs, buyers beware! Media and Internet writers are claiming—with little or no research support—that EQ can be taught, is the truest measure of human intelligence, is necessary for some career success, and is related to success in life.

Another Measure of Intelligence: Working Memory

Researchers are finding that working memory is a good predictor of verbal and non-verbal problem solving. Recent studies measuring working memory were highly correlated with scores on the verbal SAT, the Raven's Progressive Matrices test, and other tests.

Numerical Ability In Chimpanzees

Researchers are still hotly debating whether nonhuman animals are capable of symbolic representation with a richness even approaching our own abilities. Language is an obvious example of such symbol use, but the jury is still out on true language capacity in other animals. In the meantime, Sarah Boysen and her colleagues have published new research exploring the numerical representation skills of chimpanzees. While they may not be functionally equivalent to our own counting and numbering talents, they do provide a fascinating glimpse into the primate mind.

Ask Dr. Mike

- What is the "Chitterling Test?"
- What causes dyslexia?

- What is savant syndrome and what causes it?
- If Savants are so good at counting, why can't they make change for $1.00?
- Can your IQ level change over time?
- Is the term "mentally retarded" still acceptable?
- Is it possible to have a mild case of Savant Syndrome? Could this be what "gifted" really means?
- What is the longest word in the English language?

Chapter Ten
Memory

Learning Activities

Product Claims: Too Good to be True?
Miracle memory drugs, amazing weight loss programs, get rich quick schemes. They all sound too good to be true. Are they? Put your critical thinking skills to the test in working through this activity about memory drugs.

Test Your Memory
Here's your chance to test your own memory. You will play the role of an observer —an eyewitness — who is present when an embarrassing event occurs. After you observe the event, you will be asked some questions about what you remember about the event. After completing this activity, you will want to read the article by Elizabeth Loftus.

Research News

Another Measure of Intelligence: Working Memory
Researchers are finding that working memory is a good predictor of verbal and non-verbal problem solving. Recent studies measuring working memory were highly correlated with scores on the verbal SAT, the Raven's Progressive Matrices test, and other tests.

Op Ed Essays

Recovered-memory Experiences: Explaining True and False Delayed Memories of Childhood Sexual Abuse
by D. Stephen Lindsay
No issue in psychology has aroused as much passion during the 1990s as claims that, sometimes aided by therapists, people have recovered long repressed memory of horrific child abuse. Critics have responded that such memories often are recovered under conditions known to produce false memories. So who is right? Are clinicians who use "memory work" techniques "merchants of mental chaos" and a blight on

the profession of psychology? Or are critics who dispute the accuracy of recovered memories playing into the hands of child molesters?

The Psychology Place explores this issue with a <u>Scientific American Connection</u> that builds on an article by American Psychological Society President, Elizabeth Loftus, and with this helpful essay by memory researcher Stephen Lindsay, who draws on his dozen years of pertinent research, his many writings, and his conversations with people on both sides.

 ## Scientific American Connection

Creating False Memories
    by Elizabeth Loftus (1997)
Researchers are showing how suggestion and imagination can create "memories" of events that did not actually occur. (See related activity)

Emotion, Memory and the Brain
    by Joseph E. LeDoux (1994)
A sight, a smell or a chord from a melody can evoke an emotional memory. How does the brain recall such emotions? Experiments with rodents model the process. Nerve impulses from sounds that cause fear in rats have been traced along the auditory pathway to the thalamus, the cortex and the amygdala, arousing a memory that leads to a higher heart rate and the cessation of movement.

 ## Ask Dr. Mike

- If the proper cue could be found, would it be possible to retrieve any memory?
- Is any particular type of music related to memory recall in positive or negative ways? How and why?
- Can the environmental context influence memory?

Chapter Eleven
Emotion

 ## Research News

Emotion, Memory and the Brain
A sight, a smell or a chord from a melody can evoke an emotional memory. How does the brain recall such emotions? Experiments with rodents model the process. Nerve impulses from sounds that cause fear in rats have been traced along the auditory pathway to the thalamus, the cortex and the amygdala, arousing a memory that leads to a higher heart rate and the cessation of movement.

Is Embarrassment a Distinct Emotion?

What does it take before psychologists will classify a particular feeling as a distinct emotion? In much of their research on emotions, investigators have overlooked the topic of embarrassment. One research team, however, has recently ventured into this issue and concluded that the feeling is unique and definable.

 Ask Dr. Mike

- Are facial expressions reflexive?
- When I get angry, why does my chest start to hurt?
- What is a "lie detector?"

Chapter Twelve
Motivation

 Research News

Scent of a Woman: The Scientific Sequel

Many species, including humans, employ pheromones or chemical signals that convey information to and cause specific reactions in other individuals of the same species. Recent experiments have shown that the sex pheromones of female rats in estrus are both necessary and sufficient to elicit a sexual fixed action pattern in male rats, namely, penile erection. This is the first evidence of an airborne pheromone eliciting an instinctive, highly stereotyped behavioral pattern in any mammalian species.

 **Op Ed Essays**

Who or What is to Blame for the Littleton Massacre?
by Kevin Byrd, University of Nebraska at Kearney

Is there one single cause for the tragedy at Columbine High School? What do we need to know about our teenagers? Clinical psychologist Kevin Byrd proposes some answers and invites you to post your views on the forum.

 Ask Dr. Mike

- Did TV violence cause the Littleton situation?
- Do animals imitate? If so, what does this mean?

Chapter Thirteen
Theories of Personality

Learning Activities

Investigating Graphology: Is the Writing on the Wall?
Does your handwriting reveal true details of your personality? Explore the world of graphology, the art of handwriting analysis, in conjunction with the Scientific American Frontiers program, *Beyond Science*. Examine authentic writing samples, listen to a graphologist explain his craft, and do an experiment in graphology. Judge for yourself: Is graphology science or fact?

Op Ed Essays

Challenging the Nurture Assumption
Judith Rich Harris recants. She "no longer believes" much of what she has taught students through her developmental psychology textbooks. In a recent Psychological Review article (that has just been named a winner of APA Division 1's George A. Miller Award for outstanding general psychology article) and in her Free Press book *The Nurture Assumption* Harris asks, "Do parents have any important long-term effects on the development of their child's personality?" After examining the evidence, she concludes "The answer is no." Rather, genes and peer influences shape children. Thus, if we left a group of children with their same schools, neighborhoods, and peers, but switched the parents around, they would, she believes, "develop into the same sort of adults."

Scientific American Connection

The Meaning of Dreams
   by Jonathan Winson (1998)
What are we to make of all our bizarre dreams? Are they merely our brain's best attempt to make sense of random neural firing, as physiological theories have proposed? Or was Freud right that dreams are the "royal road to our unconscious"? Researcher Jonathan Winson has deftly combined elements of those and other theories with his own work to create a clearer explanation of the meaning of our dreams. (See related activity)

Ask Dr. Mike

- Can a personality test ever be "wrong"?
- What does Freud have to say about the development of homosexuality in men?
- What are inkblots made out of and how are they made?
- In the Freudian structure of the mind, is it fair to say that the Id is "selfish," and that the superego is "good"?

Chapter Fourteen
Development Over the Life Span

 Research News

All in Your Head? Attention Disorder May Be Genetic
Why is it that some children just can't seem to sit still and pay attention? Is it too much sugar, too little discipline, psychological problems, or are the causes biological? Current research suggests that attention-deficit hyperactivity disorder-ADHD-may be genetic. Imaging studies of the brain show that areas in the prefrontal and in the basal ganglia are smaller in ADHD children than non-ADHD children. Many therapies have been used to treat ADHD, but none appear to be as successful as stimulants such as Ritalin.

Fear of Death: Our Final Developmental Crisis
New research headed by psychologists at the University of Arizona lends experimental support to a theory about how people handle the fear of death. The evidence may help explain people's cultural biases toward their "own kind," especially during war time. And it tends to corroborate Freud's notion that the unconscious mind continues processing information. A self-test lets you measure your own anxiety over death and dying.

Primate Caretakers Live Longer
Overall, the parents in primate species who are invested in doing a good job in raising their young are rewarded evolutionarily by having children who survive to adulthood and possibly continue the gene line. But new research among various primate species, including humans, shows that the parent investing the greater amount of caretaking time gets an added bonus: namely, a longer life span.

Babies, Phonetics, and Mastering Language
Babies and young children are masters of language acquisition. What's behind the innate human ability to learn the sounds and meanings of spoken words in infancy, then to communicate back with increasing fluency? New research details the roles of "parentese" and "phonetic screening," and may help guide the teaching of second languages to teens and adults.

Daycare: What's a Parent to Do?
Virtually all working parents struggle with questions about daycare. When parents who must work have no other options, daycare is inevitable. Still, they worry about how long periods of time in another's care will affect their children. Research done in the 1980s indicated that extended daycare could be detrimental to the mother-child relationship, or produce more aggressive and noncompliant children. A series of recent studies, however, has changed that picture.

Dyslexia Predicted by Decreased Brain Activity
Dyslexia is a reading disorder with a cause that, for now, remains obscure. Researchers have implicated various brain areas in this distressing disorder, but their data have often been inconclusive. A recent study employing a brain imaging technique reports a very strong relationship between activity levels in a major visual pathway in the brain and the degree of dyslexia experienced by young adult subjects. It appears that a lack of proper visual functioning in the brain is, at least in part, associated with this rather common reading disability.

Birth Month Predicts Height?

A 10-year study of more than half a million males has revealed a reliable, cyclic relationship between birth month and height at age 18. The cyclicity of the height/birth month relationship trails sunshine duration by about three months: As the duration of sunshine increases, so does height, but three months later. The authors of a new paper on this phenomenon speculate that the height/birth month relationship may involve the light-sensitive hormone melatonin and its influence on the rapidly growing fetus and very young infant.

Prenatal Experience: More is Not Better

Experience begins prenatally. Researchers have been studying the effects of normal prenatal experience on development for some time and it is clear that insufficient amounts of embryonic experience can have devastating effects postnatally. A new study of precocial species shows that extra prenatal auditory experience can dramatically alter not only postnatal auditory and visual perception but mortality as well.

Should Parents Intervene in Children's Fights?

When it comes to their children's conflicts, parents face tough questions. While childcare specialists continue to debate the pros and cons of intervening, parents must decide on a daily basis whether to break up fights and how to do it fairly and wisely. A new study by Canadian researchers documented the fighting behaviors of 2-and 4-year-old children and the effects of both parental action and nonaction. Intervention, the researchers found, seemed to decrease the intensity of conflicts, while providing parents an opportunity to model invaluable conflict resolution skills.

Even Light Maternal Drinking Affects the Unborn Child

Alcohol use by a pregnant women can permanently harm the unborn fetus. Formerly, researchers thought this applied only to heavy drinkers. An accumulation of evidence, however, including some recently published, shows that even light drinking may result in cognitive and behavioral problems that seem not to improve as the child grows older. Fetal alcohol syndrome brought about by heavy drinking is the most common known cause of mental retardation, and yet it is completely preventable.

Infant Attachment, Adult Curiosity, and Cognitive Closure

Recent research has explored the relationship between people's early emotional attachments and their approach to information processing later in life. Individuals who had experienced secure relationships as infants were found to be more open to new experiences and new information than individuals who had less secure early relationships.

Childhood Attachment Style: How Stable Over the Life Span?

Attachment—the bond between parent and child—forms in infancy and continues into adulthood. Most research on attachment in adults assumes that the quality of early attachment (secure, avoidant, or ambivalent) remains relatively stable throughout the life span. But is this premise correct? A new report by Joanne Davila and coworkers at U.C.L.A. suggests that approximately 30 percent of the population change their attachment in adulthood. They found that those prone to fluctuations in adulthood tended to have insecure attachments to parents early in life. The researchers also found among the fluctuators more frequent histories of personal and family psychopathology, higher levels of personality disturbance, and a greater chance of having divorced, separated or deceased parents.

 **Op Ed Essays**

Challenging the Nurture Assumption

Judith Rich Harris recants. She "no longer believes" much of what she has taught students through her developmental psychology textbooks. In a recent Psychological Review article (that has just been named a winner of APA Division 1's George A. Miller Award for outstanding general psychology article) and in her Free Press book *The Nurture Assumption* Harris asks, "Do parents have any important long-term effects on the development of their child's personality?" After examining the evidence, she concludes "The answer is no." Rather, genes and peer influences shape children. Thus, if we left a group of children with their same schools, neighborhoods, and peers, but switched the parents around, they would, she believes, "develop into the same sort of adults."

The Power of Parents
by Jerome Kagan, Harvard University

In *The Nurture Assumption,* Judith Rich Harris argues that peers, not parents, shape children. Jerome Kagan answers Harris's challenge, noting why he believes "parents clearly do matter."

 **Scientific American Connection**

The Oldest Old
by Thomas T. Perls (1998)

People in their late nineties are often healthier and more robust than those 20 years younger. Traditional views of aging may need rethinking. (see related activity)

 Ask Dr. Mike

- What is a "critical period"?
- Is "Motherese" universal – does this appear in all cultures?
- Do young children have a conscience?
- What are the causes of various attachment styles? Is it the parent's behavior or the child's?
- If eye color is the result of a dominant (brown) allele and a recessive (blue) allele, how can you have green eyes? Using a Mendel table, the color should be either brown or blue, shouldn't it?
- If a mother smokes during pregnancy, are there any effects on the fetus?
- To what extent does the lack of infant attachment adversely influence adult behavior?
- If attachment is strong and secure at an early age, what happens when you move out on your own? Do you have to replace this secure attachment?
- We recently saw the videotape entitled "Secret of the Wild Child." This was a NOVA special featuring the unique story of the young girl who was found in California in the early 1970s after having endured almost total social isolation. My students and I were curious to know where and how Genie is today. Could you tell us what became of her?

Chapter Fifteen
Health, Stress, and Coping

 **Learning Activities**

Drug Use, Abuse and Addictions: Focus on Alcohol
In this activity, you will examine where drug abuse and addictions begin with a special focus on alcohol and its use among young people today. You will engage in a debate on lowering the drinking age and keep track of your own substance use.

 Research News

Social Control: Good and Bad for Your Health
Changing a bad habit is never easy. Friends and family may urge you to adopt healthy behaviors, such as exercising regularly, or giving up smoking; but does their urging, no matter how well-intentioned, really help? A new study of "social control" has uncovered some answers that should make loved ones reconsider their efforts.

Regrets? . . . I've Had a Few: Women's Midlife Review and Well-Being
Until recently, social scientists have tended to view midlife as a developmental stage that requires a major adaptation—especially for women who must deal with the negative stereotypes associated with aging. Contemporary studies have begun to focus on the midlives of women by examining their regrets about choices in early life and whether making relevant changes helps produce enhanced well being in midlife.

Better Living Through Mindfulness
Mindlessness, or passive information processing, can have negative physical and mental effects according to Harvard psychologist Ellen Langer. Through two decades of research, she and her colleagues have shown that mindlessness may result in prejudice against the handicapped and others, and in poor health and reduced longevity among elderly patients. Langer promotes the opposite of mindlessness, mindfulness, to improve psychological and physical well being.

Rethinking the Power of Positive Thinking
Both the popular press and research psychologists have paid substantial attention to the power of positive thinking (optimism). However, four researchers at Ohio State University have now reported that avoiding negative thinking (pessimism) may be even more important than striving for optimism when it comes to physical and psychological health. In a longitudinal study of adults, the team examined the relationships between negative life events, optimism, pessimism, and subjects' perception of their own stress, depression, anxiety, and physical health. About half of the participants were under extreme stress from caring for a relative with Alzheimer's disease. The Ohio team found that in nonstressed adults, optimism and pessimism were largely independent of each other; this was less true among the individuals coping with high stress levels. Further, it was pessimism, not optimism, that uniquely predicted psychological and physical health for both stressed and nonstressed groups. Future research is needed to determine whether the benefits of optimism accrue directly from positive thinking or from avoiding negative thinking—or perhaps some combination of the two.

Anger Sensitivity: A Hidden Cost of Child Abuse

Child abuse has been a tragic part of human history since its beginning. Only in modern times have we attempted to scientifically research the causes and effects of child abuse, as well as effective treatments. Researchers in Wisconsin and New York recently carried out important studies on children's responses to parental abuse. They showed slides of happy, angry, and neutral faces to 23 maltreated and 21 nonabused children, and simultaneously recorded their cognitive event-related potentials (ERPs), a type of brain wave. Abused children showed heightened reactivity to angry faces. This, suggest the researchers, may help explain the children's greater chances for developmental and behavioral problems.

Classes, Computers, Exams...and Beer: College Drinking

Is drinking on college campuses a serious problem? For several decades the incidence of student drinking on college campuses has been studied with mixed findings. More recent studies indicate a higher incidence of binge drinking than expected, in large mixed-sex college settings. These findings indicate that these drinking patterns are related to a higher incidence of academic, social, and legal problems. Students who binge-drink are also at risk for physical problems due to poor health related behaviors such as cigarette smoking, abuse of other substances, and unplanned sex.

Coping After Abortion

New research by Brenda Major and her colleagues explores how personal resilience, cognitive appraisals, and coping efforts work together to determine postabortion adjustment. In their longitudinal study of 527 women who underwent first-trimester abortions, they found most of the women to be well adjusted and satisfied with their decision. Women with resilient personalities appraised their experience more positively, viewing their abortion as less stressful and having confidence in their ability to cope with the abortion. Their more positive view of the experience led to more successful coping strategies. The researchers concluded that teaching more beneficial forms of coping would be a useful clinical intervention for women adjusting poorly after an abortion.

Procrastination May be Dangerous to Your Health and Performance

When facing a deadline far in the future, procrastination may succeed as a way to reduce stress. In the long run, however, procrastinators may be making themselves sick! Recent research with college students shows that those who self-identified as procrastinators early in the semester felt more stressed as a deadline approached. They also experienced more physical symptoms and visited health care professionals more often. Procrastination seems to hurt performance, too: Delaying assigned work correlated positively with lower grades on both an assigned paper and on exams.

Getting Old: Better Than You Expect

Most of us joke and worry about growing older, but many of our fears are unjustified. The authors of three articles in a recent issue of Science present data on the influence of genes, the longevity of neurons, and the fluctuations of hormones on our health as we age. Their findings are positive and their message encouraging.

Maternal Grooming: A Lifelong Aid to Stress Reduction?

Researchers at McGill University in Montreal have discovered that rats literally groom their young for success—success in resisting the negative effects of stress. High levels of maternal licking and grooming lead to adult offspring with a healthier physiological response to stress, freer tendencies to explore, and a greater ability to overcome anxiety. Are there human lessons to be learned from their maternal instincts?

Cigarette Smoking and Genetics: A Not So Unlikely Combination

Why is it easy for some people to quit smoking, while others can't seem to kick the habit? Why do some people start smoking in the first place? New research suggests that part of the answer to these questions may lie in the presence or absence of specific genes. More information about genes identified with smoking risk can ultimately identify who is at risk for nicotine dependence and can help determine the best way to quit smoking.

 **Op Ed Essays**

The Social Usefulness of Self-Esteem: A Skeptical View
by Robyn M. Dawes, Carnegie Mellon University

In pop psychology, high self-esteem is often considered a major criterion of good mental health. But does psychological science support this premise? Robyn Dawes explores the research and offers a new view of the subject of self-esteem.

Building a Positive Social Science for the 21st Century
by Martin E.P. Seligman, University of Pennsylvania

A quick search of *Psychological Abstracts* (via PsychInfo) reveals the magnitude of psychology's concern with negative states. Since 1967, 12,187 abstracts contained the keyword "fear," 41,416 mentioned "anxiety," and 54,040 mentioned "depression." Meanwhile, 313 mentioned "courage," 415 mentioned "joy," and 1,882 mentioned "happiness." Martin Seligman believes it is time for a change. In this essay, adapted from his contributions to the April 1998, APA *Monitor* and a 1998 Templeton Foundation Symposium on "Optimism and Hope," he outlines his vision for a new "positive psychology."

 **Scientific American Connection**

The Oldest Old
by Thomas T. Perls (1998)

People in their late nineties are often healthier and more robust than those 20 years younger. Traditional views of aging may need rethinking. (see related activity)

 Ask Dr. Mike

- Does stress help us to remember information (like phone numbers) or does it make us forget?
- Can meditation heal?
- I read an article recently where they said that having a "wet dream" was a normal experience and did not reflect a psychological disorder. Is this true or does it really reflect a disorder?

Chapter Sixteen
Psychological Disorders

Learning Activities

Investigating Sex Differences in Depression
Is there a gender bias in depression? Become a part of an on-line study and discover the truth. Find out your score on the Self-Rating Depression Scale and compare your results with the study averages for your gender, then see how our results compare to the national averages.

Recognizing Mood Disorders
Would you like to explore mood disorders from the clinician's chair? After a brief review of depression and mania, this activity gives you the opportunity to "diagnose" six sample patients, based on brief case histories. Includes a link to the American Psychological Association's classification of mood disorders based on DSM-IV (Diagnostic and Statistical Manual, fourth edition).

Research News

Teen Suicide—Symptom of a Changing World or Exaggerated Suggestibility in Adolescence
Suicide is one of the most frequent causes of death, worldwide, in the adolescent age group. Psychologists have explained this phenomenon in various ways, including despair for the future and an enhanced suggestibility in adolescents. A recent case of six suicides, all by hanging, of young men from the same Boston community seems to illustrate several psychological phenomena.

Editor's Note: Unabomber Update
The refusal by Kaczynski to allow an insanity defense puts that plea itself on trial: How disturbed must a person be to qualify?

The Insanity Defense and the Unabomber Trial
The trial of Unabomber suspect Theodore Kaczynski has brought the insanity defense back to public attention. Is Kaczynski a sane person who is accused of carrying out "crazy" actions or a mentally disturbed person who pretends to sanity? The insanity defense has a long but controversial history. Is it ever justified? Does "insanity" remove responsibility for a crime? How does this defense affect trial outcomes? Misconceptions about the insanity plea and its results are common, but recent scholarly articles help clear them up.

The Manic-Depressive Brain
Brain researchers using powerful imaging techniques have pinpointed an area of the brain involved in heritable forms of two relatively common mood disorders, depression and manic-depression. The brain area they observed, the subgenual prefrontal cortex, has neural connections to other brain structures involved in emotional behavior and the body's physiological responses to emotion. Finding a link between the brain region and the mood disorders may help researchers to better understand and treat those conditions in the future.

DSM-IV: How Many Entries for The Book of Names?

The Diagnostic and Statistical Manual, 4th Edition (DSM-IV), published in 1994 by the American Psychiatric Association, is our nation's main classification system for mental disorders. The book is used by mental health professionals, governmental agencies, third-party health insurers, and researchers studying disordered behavior. DSM-IV includes more than 300 disorders—nearly triple the number listed just 18 years ago in the book's first edition. Are we growing more mentally dysfunctional? Or is the classification process itself proliferating? Supporters see the burgeoning of categories as a benefit to precision research. Some critics, however, view the DSM-IV as a "marketing machine" that financially benefits practitioners but siphons off funds needed for treating the most serious mental illnesses. Recent research articles highlight the debate over the Book of Names.

Manic-Depressive Illness and Creativity
by Kay Redfield Jamison (1995)

Does some fine madness plague great artists? Several studies now show that creativity and mood disorders are linked. (See related activity)

Schizophrenic Disorder: When People Hear Voices, Who's Talking?

For many people with schizophrenic disorder, auditory hallucinations—especially of other people's voices criticizing or commanding them—are among their most distressing experiences. Several lines of recent research are helping elucidate the brain functions and cognitive processes behind these voices, as well as providing practical techniques for decreasing the discomfort of hallucinatory experiences.

Eating Disorders and Sudden Death

It has been said that a woman can never be too thin or too rich. However, sometimes excessive thinness (or the manner of achieving it) can become a death sentence for women or men. Especially in the worlds of entertainment, modeling, and sports, women often feel pressured to be thin. A recent case shows how this drive for thinness can get out of control, emphasizing the dangerous consequences of eating disorders.

Mental Illness: Dangers, Treatment, and Civil Liberties

In July 1998, two police officers were killed at the United States Capitol by Russell Weston, Jr., who had been diagnosed earlier with paranoid schizophrenia. This act again raises the question of the connection between mental illness and violence: Is there truly a connection, and if there is, how should the mentally ill be treated? What are their civil rights? Do they conflict with the greater good of the community?

The Social Consequences of Affirmative Action

Affirmative action programs have created important opportunities for individuals who experience societal discrimination and disadvantage. Such programs are controversial, however, and some have suggested that those who benefit from affirmative action also pay a price in terms of unfavorable attitudes about their capabilities. A new study by two social psychologists from Canada and Wales supports this: They examined public attitudes about a new, relatively unfamiliar, immigrant group, Surinamers, before and after exposure to a media campaign. The information they disseminated was always positive but sometimes included a mention of the group's eligibility for affirmative action. Their results show that the existence of affirmative action affects attitudes towards both the groups and specific individuals who would benefit from such programs.

Op Ed Essays

Who or What is to Blame for the Littleton Massacre?
   by Kevin Byrd, University of Nebraska at Kearney
Is there one single cause for the tragedy at Columbine High School? What do we need to know about our teenagers? Clinical psychologist Kevin Byrd proposes some answers and invites you to post your views on the forum.

Scientific American Connection

Depression's Double Standard
   by Kristen Leutwyler (1997)
Studies from 10 nations reveal that the rates of depression among women are twice as high as they are among men. Do women have a biological bent for depression, or are social double standards the major cause? (See related activity)

Ask Dr. Mike

- What is antisocial personality disorder? Can this explain the Littleton shootings?
- What is an "anxiety attack"?
- What is bi-polar disease, and how do you get it? What are some symptoms, and is there a cure?
- Can psychological blindness correct itself?
- What is the underlying cause of a phobia?
- What is Tourettes Syndrome?
- I have a history of bipolar disorder in my family. How can I tell the difference between everyday mood swings and real disorder?
- Is catharsis a good thing or a bad thing? I've heard both.
- What is "normal," anyway? If reality is based on perception, how can we label a schizophrenic as "abnormal"?
- Is it typical to feel "down" after reading or talking about depression?
- What is the likelihood that the genes for a mental disorder can be passed down from your parents? Would the home environment have any effect?
- Is it considered abnormal to sometimes have feelings of depression and consider suicide?
- With Multiple Personality Disorder, can one of the personalities be ill while the other is healthy?
- Concerning Tourette's Syndrome, does a person have inappropriate behaviors other than swearing, such as inappropriate sexual behavior in public?
- Is Anorexia Nervosa really a form of Anxiety Disorder?
- What is Luvox?

Chapter Seventeen
Approaches to Treatment and Therapy

 Research News

Feeling Low This Winter? "A Sunny Disposition" May Help
Many people experience "winter doldrums" brought on by fewer hours of daylight in the winter months. For some, however, the symptoms are more extreme and constitute a true Seasonal Affective Disorder or SAD. Young adult women are typical sufferers, but children and adolescents can show signs of SAD, as well. An effective treatment is exposure to special, very bright, lighting. Researchers are learning more about treating this disorder, as well as why it may occur.

Childhood and Adolescent Depression—To Medicate or Not?
Before 1980, few clinicians believed in childhood depression. Today, mental health professionals not only recognize depressive disorders in children but also agree that these conditions can persist and can have severe consequences. Despite the proven benefits of psychotherapy for treating childhood depression, physicians prescribed Prozac and related antidepressants to nearly 600,000 children in 1996. This represents a substantial increase over 1995 prescription levels, and it came despite a paucity of solid data on the utility and long-term effects of these relatively new drugs for young people. How should professionals make treatment decisions for depressed kids and teens?

 Ask Dr. Mike

- Is electroconvulsive therapy (ECT) always beneficial?
- I've heard that Prozac has few, if any, side effects. Is this true?
- Is it common to mix treatments for various disorders, for example, electroconvulsive therapy (ECT) and lithium?
- I am reading this book about a famous psychiatrist who sexually abused his patient under the influence of amytal. Have you ever heard of this case? What is amytal and what is it used for? What are the effects of long-term use?

Psychology on the Internet 1999–2000:
A Prentice Hall Guide

Andrew T. Stull

Adapted for Psychology by
Jeff L. Platt
North Iowa Area Community College

Contents

Preface to Psychology on the Internet   Change!   63

Introduction   O' Brave New World: Brief Internet History   65

Chapter 1   What Makes It Tick? The Basics   67
        1.1   Springs, wheels, and dials—Connecting   67
        1.2   Putting the pieces together—Organizing   70
        Activity: *The Starting Line*   72

Chapter 2   Hitting the Road: Mapping the Net   73
        2.1   Cruising the Net—Browsing   73
        2.2   Landmarks—Navigating   75
        2.3   Asking for directions—Searching   79
        Activity: *The Great Cybertrip*   82

Chapter 3   Traveling in Style: As You Like It   83
        3.1   Coffee, tea, or milk?—Customizing   83
        3.2   Wish you were here—Communicating   89
        3.3   The fun is in the going—Extending   97
        Activity: *A Talkabout Tour*   100

Appendix I   Internet Resources for Psychology   101

Appendix II   Documenting Your Electronic Sources   115

Appendix III   Evaluating Online Sources   118

Glossary   Fasten Your Seatbelts: Jargon to Go   120

Preface to Psychology on the Internet
Change!

The artist picks up the message of cultural and technological
challenge decades before its transforming impact occurs.*

Change! The original edition of this manual gasped its first breath at 7:22 p.m. on July 23, 1995. Since then, a great deal about the World Wide Web and the world at large has changed. Our world is louder, faster, and more complex than the one experienced by earlier generations. In terms of information transfer, we might be described as a techno-generation; our parents, as a paper-generation. The World Wide Web has changed as well, and it will probably continue to do so; our online future is likely to be chaotic but exciting. Prepare to revel in the difference that tomorrow will bring.

Reading this manual won't teach you all there is to know about the World Wide Web, but it will help you to teach yourself. In the future you will need to find information for yourself rather than relying solely on others, who may bear outdated knowledge. If you are successful, your skills in "cruising" the Internet will allow you to deal with ongoing change. By the end of this manual, you should be comfortable and resourceful in navigating the complexity of the Internet, from its back eddies to its thriving thoroughfares.

This manual has three chapters. In the Introduction, *O' Brave New World*, we will describe the origin of and the innovations behind the Internet. In Chapter 1, *What Makes It Tick?*, we will explain the use of a Web browser and describe how you can connect to the Internet. The boxed and end-of-chapter exercises will give you practice in using your browser as well as introduce you to some of the wonderful places on the Internet.

In Chapter Two, *Hitting the Road*, you'll learn more about how to use your browser in order to cruise the endless byways of the Internet. Also, you will be introduced to resources and strategies for information searching. The boxed and end-of-chapter exercises will reinforce your navigational skills and give you practice in searching for some of the great Psychology and Psychology-related sites on the Internet. These resources, along with related newsgroups, appear in Appendix I.

In Chapter Three, *Traveling in Style*, you will learn how to customize your Web browser to make it more responsive to your needs. You will find yourself changing from an observer into an enthusiastic Internet participant. The boxed and end-of-chapter exercises will help you contact others on the Internet.

Internet resources are listed in Appendix I, and Appendices II and III discuss documenting and evaluating online sources. Finally, a glossary defines the buzzwords.

*After each major heading, you'll see a quote from *Understanding Media, The Extensions of Man* (MIT Press, Cambridge, MA, 1964) by Marshall McLuhan. See also "McLuhan Meets the Net," by Larry Press, Communications of the ACM, July 1995.

Introduction
O' Brave New World
Brief Internet History

As electrically constructed, the globe is no more than a village.

This thing that we now call the Internet has been evolving ever since it was first developed over twenty-five years ago. Many people have compared the Internet to a living creature because of the way it grows and changes. You may find its history quite interesting.

In the late 1950s and early 1960s, scientists and engineers realized the importance of sharing information and communicating through their computers. Many different groups attempted to develop computer network languages that would enable computers to exchange information with one another. But unfortunately, all of these computer systems used different languages—people on different systems still had difficulty communicating with one another. It was like the Tower of Babel all over again.

The Internet was born as the solution to this problem. The U.S. government paid for the development of a common network language, called a protocol, which was eventually shared freely. Over time, many formerly isolated networks from all over the world adopted this language. Thus, the best description of the Internet is that it is not a network, but a network of networks. However, the Internet is independent of governments and regulation—there is no central Internet agency. Change is spurred by the common needs of the people that use the Internet.

Admittedly, this type of network system isn't the most graceful—but it works. If you saw a diagram of this great big computer network, you might find it resembles a spider's web. On this web, information can travel between any two points along any one of many possible paths.

Originally, the chief purpose of the Internet was to provide a distribution system for scientific exchange and research. Gradually, however, the Internet also became a digital post office, enabling people to send mail and transfer computer files electronically. Although the Internet is still used extensively by scientists, the commercial sector is currently the most powerful force behind its growth.

As technology changed, the speed with which information could be transferred and the way we viewed information changed. In 1991, an important new user interface was developed at the University of Minnesota: the *Gopher*. *Gopher* is a visually-oriented search tool for the Internet that allows users to locate information found on other computers. Because of *Gopher*, and other, more sophisticated *graphical user interfaces* developed since 1991, it is now possible to search through vast stores of information on computers all over the world. Once the desired information is found, it can be easily downloaded to the user's computer. Amazing if you think about it! You could be on your computer in Shepherdstown, West Virginia, and view information from London, Mexico City, or Tokyo without even realizing it. Wham! And no airline tickets!

In 1992, researchers in Switzerland helped to create a new format for information exchange that led to the explosive growth of the World Wide Web (WWW). Information on the Web is posted as a "page" that may contain text, images, sounds, and even movies. The organization of a page is much like any printed page in a book. However, Web pages make use of *hypermedia*. Hypermedia involves the use of words and images as links, or connecting points, between different texts, images, sounds, or movies on other computers throughout the world. *Hypertext* Web pages contain links only to other text documents.

However, the introduction of the Web created a dilemma: It was a great place to go, but there was no easy way to get there. We still lacked a convenient software program that would allow users to access the Web easily. In 1993, a program called *Mosaic* was developed by the National Center for Supercomputing Applications (NCSA). It allowed the user to browse Web pages as well as use other Internet resources such as electronic mail (e-mail).

In 1991, around 700,000 people were using the Internet. After the introduction of *Mosaic*, users increased to around 1.7 million. Upon the release of Netscape *Navigator*, users were estimated at 3.2 million. Since then, the growth hasn't slowed much—various estimates suggest that the number of people who have access to the Internet ranges from 20 million to 100 million.

Just listen to the popular media. When was the last time you saw a television program, heard a radio commercial, or read a magazine without encountering something about the Internet? Today, you have access to animation, video clips, audio files, and even virtual reality worlds. Imagine all the new ways we will be able to view tomorrow's digital world.

For those of you who already have some Web experience, here are a few Web addresses discussing the history and growth of the Internet. Simply type the address into your Web browser exactly as it appears below. If you are just beginning to learn about the Internet, you might want to visit these sites after you learn more about Web browsers and Internet addresses in Chapter 2.

BBN Timeline
BBN includes an Internet history timeline. It places the important Internet events in context with other historical events and throws in plenty of social commentary to give you perspective.
Address: http://www.bbn.com/timeline/

Hobbes' Internet Timeline
Hobbes' site offers a great deal about the Internet, the people who use it, and online culture.
Address: http://info.isoc.org/guest/zakon/Internet/History/HIT.html

Netizens: On the History and Impact of Usenet and the Internet
This is a comprehensive collection of essays about the history, nature, and impact of the Internet.
Address: http://www.columbia.edu/~hauben/netbook/

Chapter 1
What Makes It Tick?
The Basics

An Indian is the servomechanism of his canoe,
as the cowboy of his horse or the executive of his clock.

Many of you reading this manual have a lot of experience with computers, while others have little or none. In the first section of this chapter, we will briefly describe the basic computer setup you'll need, how to use a modem, and choose an Internet Service Provider (ISP). Many of you may have computers on your campus that are set up to allow Internet access. In case you don't, we'll list the minimum in terms of systems, connections, and services that you'll need for the Internet.

In the second section of this chapter, we will explain some of the idiosyncrasies of the Internet and describe the general features of most Internet browser software. A popular Web browser, Netscape *Navigator* or *Communicator*, is used to illustrate discussions. Another popular browser is Microsoft *Internet Explorer*. We will refer to the 4.0 version of both browsers; they are the two clear frontrunners in user popularity. However, as of March 18, 1999, Microsoft announced the release of its 5.0 version of *Internet Explorer*; *Navigator* is sure to respond with its own updated version soon enough. But as of now the 4.0 versions are stable, widely accepted, and *free* to students. We don't advocate any particular browser; you will probably want to try various browsers and make up your own mind. Although our illustrations focus on *Navigator*, fear not; browsers share many of the same features. When necessary, we will point out the particulars of *Internet Explorer*. We are going to describe the features of both browsers as they pertain to the PC versions. The Macintosh versions of *Navigator* and of *Internet Explorer* have slightly different menus and layouts, but once you've learned the basic techniques, it's easy to switch back and forth between browsers and platforms.

Section 1.1
Springs, wheels, and dials—Connecting

What is the difference between a Rolex and a Timex? Without much consideration, the main difference is the price. But if we consider how well each of these watches meets our basic need for being on time, the two watches are very similar. The same goes for computers and networks. The simple no-frills components will save you money; the high-gloss gear will transform your cash into dash and make your Internet browsing only a little more enjoyable.

To get started, you'll need a *computer*, a *modem*, an *Internet connection*, and *browser software*. The descriptions that follow will help you understand each component and its function to access the Internet.

The Computer
Be careful how you approach this issue if you ask someone for advice on which computer to buy. Many people have strong opinions about the differences between Macintosh and PC-compatible systems. The best advice that we can give to you is to test them both at a computer store. Choose the one that you can pay for and are most comfortable using.

These are the *minimum* system configurations that you'll need:

PC-Compatible
- Intel 486
- Windows 3.1
- VGA monitor
- 16 MB of RAM
- 8 MB of free disk space for browser software

Macintosh
- 68030
- MacOS 7.0
- 256 color monitor
- 16 MB of RAM
- 8 MB of free disk space for browser software

If you are purchasing a new computer, the minimum may not be readily available and therefore is not recommended. Stepping up to a PowerMac (with MacOS 7.6 or higher) or a Pentium-based PC (with Windows 9x) would be more desirable.

A new innovation is the Network Computer, or NC. An NC is a computer without all of the software that you expect in an ordinary computer: word processing, drawing, graphing, and number crunching. Because these features may be helpful to you, you should consider the purchase of an NC carefully. An NC (a box that sits on top of your TV) will allow you to connect your television directly to the Internet. *Web*TV is currently the most popular, but we suspect that you'll see many different brands in the future. The advantage of such products is that they are much cheaper than an ordinary (but more capable) computer. Also, you don't have to be a computer whiz to use them.

The Modem

You probably want to know why you need a modem if you already have a computer. A modem is a device that MOdulates and DEModulates—that is, it translates a computer signal into a telephone signal, and vice versa. Although computers and telephones were set up to speak different "languages," you can use a modem to translate between your computer and another computer across your telephone line. Modems come in different "sizes," so don't just go out and buy the cheapest one on sale. Definitely don't buy one from a garage sale unless you really know what you're doing. Because modem technology changes so quickly, older equipment may be useful only as a doorstop. The number one thing that you need to know about a modem is its speed of transmission. Modem speeds are referred to in units called baud (a bit is a basic unit of digital information and a baud is the speed of transmitting 1 bit in 1 second). At one time a modem speed of 2600 baud was considered adequate. However, the minimum speed requirements have been steadily increasing as users demand more information at faster rates. You should purchase a modem with a speed of at least 28,800 baud (28.8K baud). With a 28.8K baud modem you can expect that it will take a few seconds to transfer a typical Web page. However, keep in mind that manufacturers will continue to introduce newer and faster modems as pages become more complex and as users demand faster speeds. If you are about to purchase a modem, the standard speed as of this writing is 56k. Connect to **http://www.miningco.com** and punch in the word "modems" into the search engine for the latest on buying a new modem. (We'll talk more about search engines a bit later but this site is very useful for all types of research.)

You also need to make sure that your modem will work with your computer's operating system. Generally, this isn't a big deal, as all modems are basically the same and top manufacturers produce software for all of the major operating systems. Just remember to read the box to make sure it contains the software you need. Included with the software is an installation manual and a phone number to a help desk. If you run into trouble, don't hesitate to try both. As for which brand of modem to purchase, buy what you can afford. Your Internet Service Provider or your campus computer administrator may recommend a particular brand of modem. Take this suggestion seriously. The technicians within your ISP or campus are likely to be familiar with the recommended modem and will be able to help you if problems arise.

The word modem may also refer to a device that allows you to connect your computer or television to a service line. By the time this guide is published, you will undoubtedly hear of things called ISDN modems and cable modems. An ISDN modem is a classic misnomer because the ISDN signal is already understood by computers and isn't modulated and doesn't need to be demodulated. The cable modem refers to a box that connects between your cable TV line (not your telephone line) and your computer or television.

The Internet Connection

Your campus may already be using the Internet as a teaching and learning tool. If not, there are many resources to help you set up a connection from home.

Some campuses, although lacking a walk-in lab, have made arrangements for students to dial into the campus computer system and connect to the Internet with a modem. If this is the case, search out the campus computer guru and ask for help.

Another option is to subscribe to a company such as *America Online, CompuServe, Microsoft Network,* or one of the many independent Mom and Pop companies currently offering monthly access to the Internet. It is a buyer's market and you should shop around. Test drive everything before you buy. This will save you a great deal of frustration. Here are a few things to consider when choosing an Internet Service Provider:

Does the ISP have a local number for your area? You need to call the provider each time you access the Internet. Paying a toll call every time you do so will become costly if you use the Internet regularly.

Can their system handle a large number of simultaneous connections? Ask them how many users they can handle at one time and how many subscribers they have. Although they may have a reasonable price and a local number, it doesn't mean much if you can't get on to use it. If after you subscribe you find that you are never able to connect or that the only available access is late at night or early in the morning, find a new ISP.

Do they offer SLIP/PPP connections? This is the type of connection that you'll need if you want to use a graphical browser like Navigator or Internet Explorer. Some ISPs only offer shell accounts. Shell accounts require you to type in each command as you would with a command-line interface such as provided in DOS. It is somewhat like driving a horse and buggy when everyone else has an automobile.

Do they have a reasonable monthly subscription fee? Cheapest is not always best. The added features and the staffing support are important points to consider when choosing a service. Some Internet Service Providers offer you unlimited monthly connect time for a flat fee and others charge for a specific number of hours per month (with hourly rates thereafter). Estimate your expected usage and purchase accordingly. Ask if there is a fee to upgrade your service if you find that you need more time. If you have a roommate, consider upgrading the service and splitting the cost. This may save you money.

Does your ISP include the Internet browser software in the price? You'll find that not all do. Most ISPs have an agreement with either Netscape or Microsoft to bundle their browser software. The provided software may also be partially configured to work on the ISP's system. Moreover, the technicians will be better able to help you with a problem.

Is the ISP a regional or local company? This may not be important to everyone, but some of you may go home during holidays and vacations. If the ISP covers a wider area, then you can still check your e-mail and cruise the Net when you are away from school.

Do they have a help line in case you need technical assistance to set up your connection? Call the help line before you subscribe and make sure you get a real person. Although you may be asked to leave your name and number, you should expect to get a return call within 24 hours. If they don't return your call within this period, then the service is probably understaffed or poorly managed.

Does the ISP offer both newsgroup and e-mail access in addition to a connection to the Web? This is usually standard but there are always exceptions.

Does it cost you extra for additional e-mail addresses? If you have a roommate, then you may find that it is more affordable to split the cost of a subscription and pay for an additional e-mail account.

Will your ISP add newsgroups at your request? Most ISPs subscribe to a small fraction of the available newsgroups and you may find that they don't include some of the basic, academic groups that your instructors may recommend. It shouldn't cost anything for the ISP to add these groups to their list.

Does the ISP offer you space for your own Web page? Often, one of the features offered in the basic package is the option of posting your own homepage. A limited amount of memory will be provided by the ISP.

The most important thing to remember when using an ISP is to expect courteous and prompt service. If you don't like what you are paying for, then cancel and go somewhere else. There are plenty of competitors willing to offer you better service.

The Browser Software

A descriptive name for software such as *Navigator* or *Internet Explorer* is *browser* software, because that is what most people do with it. It is used to browse or wander, sometimes aimlessly, through the Internet.

Many Web browsers are on the market today, and new ones frequently enter the race to capture your dollar.

All browsers have advantages and disadvantages. You should evaluate several and choose the one that is most comfortable for you. (However, when choosing a browser, remember that seeing over the dashboard is all that is really important. Don't get wrapped up in features that you'll never use.) *Navigator, Internet Explorer*, and many of the other browsers are free for student use! Don't be afraid to look at several. At the end of the chapter you will find several Web addresses that offer such software. Of course, if you purchase the browser at the store, you also get a user's manual, which you don't get with the free, educational copy.

If you have all of these basic elements and they've been put together correctly, you should be ready to surf. (See the activity at the end of this chapter, *The Starting Line*.) The rest of this manual is devoted to guiding you through some of the wonderful places that will allow you to enjoy the depth and scope of Psychology.

Section 1.2
Putting the pieces together—Organizing

The software that you'll use to access the Net is commonly called a *client* or a Web *browser*. It functions according to an information exchange model called the *client-server model* (Figure 1.1). In this way, a *client* (your Web browser software) communicates with a server (a computer with Web server software) on the Internet to exchange information. When referring to the Web, the information that your browser receives from the server is called a page.

What really appears on these Web pages? The best way to find out is to see for yourself. Sit down in front of a computer, start your browser software, and connect to the Internet. Your browser is proba-

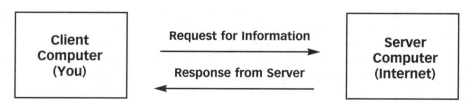

Figure 1.1. The client requests information from the server. The requested information is displayed on the client computer.

bly already set to start at a specific page. This start page is often referred to as a *homepage*. Web pages usually include both text and images. Some also use sounds and videos. The use of different information types is called multimedia. A basic rule of the road is that anything that can be saved or recorded onto a computer can be distributed on the Internet through a Web page.

When you choose a page it will be sent to your computer. After the requested information has been sent by the server, your computer will display it for you. However, sometimes the Internet is not as responsive as you'd like. (Why do you think some people refer to the World Wide Web as the World Wide Wait?) A few analogies and real-world considerations may help you see why this is so.

Patchwork Quilts

The patchwork quilt you might use during cold nights is one analogy. The quilt may have been crafted by your grandmother. Or in another time, a community of women (not all with equal sewing talent) may have met to produce a single quilt from a collection of patches differing in color, shape, and pattern. Due to the complexity, age, use, care, and variations in craftsmanship, quilts eventually become threadbare and require mending. The Internet is just like your favorite quilt in this respect.

Spider Webs

As we mentioned in the introduction, the Internet can be thought of as a big spider web. If you're the spider and you're trying to get to a fly stuck in the web, you usually have more than one path to get there. Some paths are more direct than others, but there are choices. Like a spider web, sometimes a small section of the Internet drops out of the "Web" and traffic has to be rerouted. This obviously causes increased traffic on the remaining strands, which in turn increases your waiting time.

Far Away Places

Remember that the Internet mimics the real world. Distance is a factor in determining how long it takes to access a Web page. Generally, loading a page from a machine across town is much faster than loading a page from across the nation or across the world.

Time Zones and Lunch

The world works on different time zones and the Internet does too. And what about lunch? Most people in the Western world take lunch around noon, and many of them check their e-mail or browse the Web as well. You can usually expect Internet traffic to be slow during that time. Let's now consider the distance factor. There is a three-hour time difference between the East and West coasts of North America, so the lunch rush lasts about four hours. Your location will determine if you are on the lead, middle, or tail end of the rush. Plan accordingly.

Parking Lots

Surfing the Web can be like shopping during the holidays. You either arrive early or park a few miles away. Here's the connection: A transaction occurs between your computer and another when you load a Web page for viewing. You require a document (a Web page) from somewhere on the Internet (a server). Obviously, a slow connection to the Internet on the client side may cause delays. But consider what is happening on the server end of the transaction. Small, slow servers will take longer to serve Web pages than large, fast servers. Now think about the holiday rush: Although there is normally adequate parking, a holiday sale and a limited number of parking spaces can add hours to your shopping. It should not be difficult to see how large, fast servers can be rapidly overloaded if they are hosting a really interesting Web site.

When Microsoft released an updated version of Internet Explorer, over twenty state-of-the-art machines went down because of excessive demand. Basically, Microsoft's parking lot wasn't big enough for the shopping rush.

By this time, you probably understand enough about each of the basic components of an Internet to try it out. Even if you're feeling unsure, don't worry. You don't need to know everything there is to know about each component. And you can always learn more from the user's guides provided by the manufacturers. Just take it one step at a time and you'll piece everything together.

Activity:
The Starting Line

There's no better time than now to get started. And you really don't need a destination to have fun. This activity is intended to help you get ready to cruise or surf the Internet. Even if you don't have a computer to access the Internet, use a friend's computer or one on campus to view this material.

The Browser
You should have a computer and a modem. Use the following Internet addresses to research the right browser for you.

> **Netscape**
> http://www.netscape.com
> **Microsoft**
> http://www.microsoft.com
> **Browserwatch**
> http://browserwatch.internet.com

The Internet Service Provider
With your computer, modem, *and* browser, you're only one step away. Use the following Internet addresses to research the right ISP for you.

> **Choosing the Internet Service Provider (Netscape)**
> http://home.netscape.com/assist/isp_select/index.html
> **Internet Access Provider Guide**
> http://www.liii.com/~dhjordan/students/docs/welcome.htm
> **Choosing An Internet Provider**
> http://tcp.ca/Dec95/Commtalk_ToC.html
> **Internet Service Providers by Area Code**
> http://thelist.internet.com

Research
It's always nice to have an independent opinion; therefore, read what the critics have to say. The following Internet addresses are for two of the largest publishers of computer-related magazines. Between them, they print nearly 50 different popular periodicals about computers and the Internet. Search their databases for articles that will help you make Internet decisions. You can read the articles online.

> **CMP Media** (Publisher of *Windows Magazine* and others)
> http://www.techweb.com/info/publications/publications.html
> **Ziff Davis** (Publisher of *PC Magazine*, *MacWEEK*, and others)
> http://www5.zdnet.com/findit/search.html

Chapter 2
Hitting the Road
Mapping the Net

*Under electronic technology the entire business of man
becomes learning and knowing.*

By now, you should be prepared to see the world, or at least the World Wide Web. In this chapter, you'll develop a better understanding of the browser as a tool for navigating the Internet. The first section discusses basic navigation techniques; the second describes how to read Internet addresses; and the third introduces you to some of the information tools available on the Internet for finding your way around.

Section 2.1
Cruising the Net—Browsing

Even though the Internet is vast, finding your way around is no harder than finding your way to a friend's house. Information on the Internet has an address just as your friends do. Most browsers allow you to type in an address and thereby access information, or "go to" a particular document.

The two most common browsers are Netscape *Navigator* and Microsoft *Explorer*. Let's take a look at how to enter an address using the Web browser Netscape *Navigator*, shown in Figure 2.1. Start by finding the text entry box, which is located to the right of the word *Location*. (Sometimes the word *Netsite* or *Address* is used instead.) If you have *Navigator* (or *Explorer*), type in the address and press the return button on your keyboard.

Now take a look at the row of boxes directly above the text box. Each one contains an icon; together, they are known as the *tool bar*. Clicking on an individual box causes the computer to execute the command in the box.

How do each of these commands help you navigate the Internet? Let's return to our analogy. Suppose you go to a friend's new home for a party but forget the house-warming present. What do you do? Drive home, of course. A Web browser will let you do something similar. In Figure 2.1, find the button labeled *Back*—it's at the far left. By clicking on this button you can return to the Web page you just visited. If you have gone to many Web pages, you can use it repeatedly to make your way back to your starting point.

Here's the address of a site you might want to visit. The Associated Press and *US News and World Report* provide free news services. You can reach them at the following addresses:

http://wire.ap.org

http://www.usnews.com/usnews/home.htm

Now find the *Home* button. By selecting this button, you will immediately return to the homepage configured for your browser. When you first begin using your browser, it will be set to a page determined by the company that created it.

Figure 2.1. The tool bar for Netscape *Navigator* offers basic navigation features such as *Back*, *Forward*, and *Home*. You will find everything you'll need to navigate around the Internet.

Two other buttons common to most browsers are *Stop* and *Reload* (this button is called *Refresh* in *Explorer*). *Stop* is pretty easy to understand but *Reload/Refresh* needs just a bit more explanation. As you explore more of the Internet, you'll realize that complete pages don't show up in your browser window instantly. Instead, different types of elements (pictures, icons, text, animations, etc.) appear over time as they are moved from the server to your browser. Occasionally, you'll notice that a page loads without some of these elements. This is often caused by an error in the transmission. Use the *Reload/Refresh* button to request a new copy of the page.

You don't always have to know the address of a page to view it. The wonderful thing about the Web is that you can access pages through the use of hyperlinks. You will notice that hyperlinks are often colored (typically blue) and underlined words on a Web page. Images may also be hyperlinks. Your mouse is used to select or click on the desired hyperlink. Some Web authors write their pages so that their hyperlinks are hidden from you. If you aren't sure where the hyperlinks are, just click on everything. You can't break anything. Clicking on a hyperlink will take you to a new Web page just as typing in an address does.

Here are a few more places you might find both fun and interesting.

The Louvre Museum in Paris
   http://www.paris.org/Musees/Louvre/

The Internet Movie Database
   http://us.imdb.com/

MTV Online
   http://www.mtv.com/

Top Secret Recipes on the Web
   http://www.topsecretrecipes.com/

Welcome to the Dilbert Zone
   http://www.unitedmedia.com/comics/dilbert/

Experiment with each of the tool bar buttons on your browser. Remember that you can always use your *Back*, *Forward,* or *Home* buttons to retrace your steps.

The author of a Web page can connect *one* image to *many* different places. This type of hyperlink is sometimes called a *clickable map*. For example, think of a Web page with a map of an archaeological dig. The creator of such a document could place a hyperlink at various locations on the map so that your selection of these locations would take you to different information about the artifacts that were found there. For a little experience in using this type of navigation, visit the sites in the following box.

Here are three addresses that use clickable maps. They are also good places to find helpful information on psychological topics.

The Visible Embryo
http://www.visembryo.com/baby/index.html

U.S. Department of Health and Human Services Home Page
http://www.os.dhhs.gov

Internet Psychology Lab
http://kahuna.psych.uiuc.edu/ipl/index.html

Not all browsers support clickable maps. Most experienced Web authors, however, provide conventional hyperlinks to related sites in addition to the clickable map.

Some Web pages contain *forms*. A form is generally a request for information, which you may respond to by clicking with your mouse or typing an answer. Forms can be used to survey users, answer questions, or make requests. As the box below shows, you can obtain valuable information from companies, government agencies, or educational institutions.

Experiment with the following links which involve forms. Not all browsers support forms, so you will need to determine if yours does. However, if you are using the 4.0 or higher versions of *Navigator* or *Explorer*, you should be fine.

Votelink: The Voice of the Net
http://www.votelink.com/

Health Risk Assessment
http://www.youfirst.com/hra.htm

MSNBC Body Mass Calculator
http://www.msnbc.com/modules/quizzes/bmicalc.asp

The Great American Website
http://www.uncle-sam.com

Time-Life's Virtual Garden Electronic Encyclopedia
http://pathfinder.com/VG/

Section 2.2
Landmarks—Navigating

The Internet addresses that you've been using are also called *Uniform Resource Locators*, or *URLs*. Each URL (pronounced "earl") has a couple of basic parts just like a residential address. Look at some of the URLs that you've used already. Do you notice any similarities among them?

Here is another typical URL (this will take you to a pretty cool site). The three basic components of an URL are listed below the address. Compare this one to the others you've seen so far.

http://www.illusionworks.com/html/jump_page.html

protocol	http://
server	www.illusionworks.com
path	/html/jump_page.html

You may notice that some addresses don't have a path element—this information is not always necessary. Be careful when you type an URL. Even one incorrect letter will prevent the browser from finding the desired site. Here is an additional resource if you'd like to learn more about Internet addresses:

http://www.ncsa.uiuc.edu/demoweb/url-primer.html

Now pick up any recent magazine and leaf through the articles and advertisements. With little effort you should be able to recognize a few more URLs. Just as you might recognize a string of numbers to be a phone number (e.g., 555-1212), you should be able to spot URLs by their characteristic form and order. An URL may seem confusing at first glance, but think of it as a postal address strung together without any spaces.

The *protocol* of the URL indicates how the information is stored. In the last box, http refers to the protocol, or language, that is used by all Web servers. The colon and slashes are used to separate it from the name of the server. They are not necessarily present in every type of URL. The *path* describes the location of the Web page on the server.

Up to this point, we have only been discussing browsers as way of navigating through information using hyperlinks. However, browsers also have the power to link to other, much older, formats of information. Try the following URLs to notice how the information differs. Although the Gopher sites are a dying breed on the Internet, you can still search for such sites at: **http://galaxy.einet.net/GJ/index.html**. Examples of such formats are as follows:

ftp://mapping.usgs.gov/pub/ti/DEM/demguide/

gopher://vmsgopher.cua.edu./11gopher_root_eric_ae:[_tc]

HTTP, FTP, and Gopher are not the only protocols, but they are the three you're most likely to encounter. Have you ever encountered the following Internet protocols?

telnet://

wais://

news:

A domain is just a fancy name for a functional network group. The last part of the server name defines the domain to which the server belongs. The most common domain is indicated by the letters edu; all educational institutions are members of this domain group. Another important domain is com, which stands for commercial and includes Internet servers that belong to **commercial** companies. You are also likely to encounter domains that serve other groups; abbreviations for a few of these are shown below.

Here are some URLs that may help expand your understanding of domains. Can you determine what each domain group represents?

http://zzyx.ucsc.edu/~dreams/

http://www.nasa.gov

http://www.dtic.mil

http://www.randi.org/

http://www.taconic.net/seminars/fas02.html

The first address suggests that surfing can be quite unpredictable. Don't say we didn't warn you.

In your travels, you will eventually jump to a server that is outside your country. Much, but not all, of the information on these servers is in English. URLs of servers outside the United States have an additional section at the end of the server name. It is a two letter code that indicates the country. Here are just a few examples of the many you might find. (All the country codes are listed in **http://www.ics.uci.edu/pub/websoft/wwwstat/country-codes.txt**)

- .au   Australia
- .ca   Canada
- .ch   Switzerland
- .nl   Netherlands
- .lt   Lithuania
- .pe   Peru
- .uk   United Kingdom

Here is yet another opportunity to encounter new places on the Web. It is a directory that allows you to search for specific things. This group of tools is discussed later in the chapter, but you might want to play with it first.

Yahoo!

http://www.yahoo.com

Remember that you won't break anything. If you get lost, you can always shut down the program, have lunch, and try again later!

Return Visit

Now that you've found a number of interesting pages, how do you find them again a day or a week later? Your browser provides a way to mark an intriguing site and quickly return to it.

Navigator

Navigator uses the feature called *Bookmarks* to compile a list of pages you frequently visit. Figure 2.2 will give you an idea of what this feature looks like. When you wish to return to one of these pages, you simply select it from the list by clicking on it with your mouse. You will jump directly to the site.

Here is an URL to get your collection started. Try this address: **http://www.hotwired.com**. It's a pretty interesting place: the online version of Wired Magazine. Select *Add Bookmark* from the *Bookmarks* menu (see Figure 2.2) which appears either to the left of the *Location* window or under the

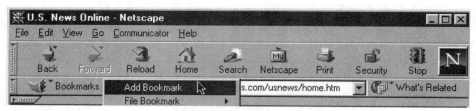

Figure 2.2. As pages are added to this list they will appear in the *Bookmarks* menu.

Communicator/Bookmarks/Add Bookmark menu. Later on, if you use your mouse to select the *Bookmarks* menu, you'll see that *Hotwired* is just a jump away. Thus, you don't have to memorize the URL or haphazardly jump around until you find it again.

Explorer

Explorer uses a feature called *Favorites* to compile a list of pages you frequently visit. When you wish to return to one of these pages, you simply select it from the list by clicking on it with your mouse. You will jump directly to the site. Here is an URL to get your collection started. Try this address: **http://www.hotwired.com**. It's a pretty interesting place: the online version of Wired Magazine. Select *Add to Favorites. . .* from the Favorites menu. Later on, if you use your mouse to select the *Favorites* menu, you'll see that *Hotwired* is just a jump away. Thus, you don't have to memorize the URL or haphazardly jump around until you find it again.

Now that you've got the hang of it, give the following URLs a try.

Links to ESPN SportsZone, WNBA, and More
http://www.starwave.com

Independent Underground Music Archive
http://www.iuma.com

Airline, Car, and Hotel Reservations
http://www.travelocity.com/

World Lecture Hall
http://www.utexas.edu/world/lecture/index.html

TicketMaster Online
http://www.ticketmaster.com

Internet Plaza
http://internet-plaza.com

Siskel and Ebert Movie Reviews
http://www.tvplex.com/BuenaVista/SiskelAndEbert

Dealer Car Prices
http://www.edmunds.com/

Bartlett's Familiar Quotations
http://www.columbia.edu/acis/bartleby/bartlett/

Electronic Postcards
http://persona.www.media.mit.edu/postcards/

Weird Sites
http://www.deiman.nl/weird/

Online Parenting
http://www.parentsplace.com/

Navigator

The *Edit Bookmarks* option allows you to organize your Web address list. When you select this option, a small window will open; in it you can move and manipulate your list of Web addresses.

Explorer

To organize your Web address list using *Explorer*, use the option called *Organize Favorites* on the toolbar. When you select this option, a small window will open; in it you can move and manipulate your list of Web addresses.

Travel History

If you've been working along with your manual and browser at the same time, you've probably been to many places on the Web. If you want to move back and forth between your selections, you're probably using the *Forward* and *Back* buttons on the browser toolbar. But what do you do if you want to go back to some place you've visited fifteen jumps ago? Do you press the *Back* button fifteen times? Well, it works, but it's a little slow. You might want to try a new feature: It allows you to jump rapidly to any of the places you've visited along your path of travel.

Navigator

Select the *Go* menu. You'll see a list of all of the places you've visited on your journey. To jump to a site on the list, simply click/select the site with your mouse. You'll also find a similar feature called *History* under the *Communicator* menu. By selecting *History*, you'll open a new window listing the names *and* the URLs for all of the places you've visited recently. Because the list compiled under *Go* or *History* begins anew each time you start your browser, you should use *Bookmarks* when you find something interesting.

Explorer

Select the *History* button on the tool bar or on the left-hand side of the Web window. You'll see the places you've visited on your journey. To jump to a site on the list, simply click/select the site with your mouse. Although the default setting causes the list compiled under *History* to begin anew each time you start your browser, you can change that setting to keep pages in history. To do so, choose *Internet Options* from the *View* menu. A pop-up window with tabbed pages will appear. Choose the *General* tab and on the bottom you'll find a box indicating the number of days pages will be kept in history. Simply insert the number of days, click on *Apply*, then close the window, and you'll be set.

Section 2.3
Asking for directions—Searching

The Internet is full of valuable information, but it's not always easy to find what you need. A number of easy-to-use tools are available for free. With practice, these tools will help you develop your information-finding skills.

There are two types of tools that you'll use most often to search for information. These are *Directories* and *Search Engines*.

Directories

Yahoo! (**http://www.yahoo.com**) is only one of many directories that are available on the Internet, but it is the best one available for general topics. (The name Yahoo is taken from Jonathan Swift's *Gulliver's Travels*, which describes a Yahoo as a crude, uncivilized, and according to one of *Yahoo's* founders, an interesting person.)

Yahoo! began as a simple listing of information by category, kind of like a card catalog. In the last few years, it has added the ability to search for specific information. At the top level of the directory, there are several very general categories, but as you move deeper into the directory you'll notice that the categories become more specific. To find information, you simply choose the most appropriate category at the top level and continue through each successive level until you find what you're looking for (or until you realize you're in the wrong place). It's not unusual to get lost. In such cases, just begin again and try different categories.

Suppose that you're taking a child development course and want to find information on a specific topic (such as spina bifida) for a research paper. Within *Yahoo!*, notice that two of the level categories are *Health* and *Science*. Since the *Health* category includes *Medicine* and *Diseases* it would seem to be the most appropriate place to find information on the topic, so give it a try. Note, however, that you could also search *Biology* in *Science*. Searching for *spina bifida* under *Health,* you'll get over 41 "hits" (or site matches). Don't celebrate yet. If you examine these hits, you'll see that not all of them contain the information you want. These sites may be interesting to visit but they may not give you the information you need for a research paper in a typical Child Development class. Because *Yahoo!* cross-references among the categories, you'll find that several related categories will lead to the information you desire.

Much of your success in finding information using a directory like *Yahoo!* centers around your preparation for the search. Often, it is possible to find information on a topic in a category that may at first seem unrelated to your topic of interest. Again, let's take the example of spina bifida. Are you interested in the personal side of living with spina bifida or are you more interested in the medical literature? Even if you are more concerned about finding information from the medical field, a quick investigation of a site concerning an individual's experience of having spina bifida may contain links to other sites that contain the information you desire.

Prepare yourself for a search *before* you jump into one. In the long run, it will save you both time and frustration. Don't be afraid to try some unusual approaches in your search strategy. A good technique is to pull out your thesaurus and look up other names for the topic you're searching. Think of everything associated with your question and give each of these possibilities a try. You never know what might turn up a gold mine.

Search Engines

A more direct approach to finding information on the Web is to use a *search engine*, which is a program that runs a search while you wait for the results. Many search engines can be found on the Web. Some of Web search engines are commercial and may charge you a fee to run a search. Search engines are also available for other parts of the Internet: *Archie, Veronica,* and *Jughead* are examples of such search engines.

Alta Vista (**http://www.altavista.digital.com**) offers general and detailed searches through what Digital Equipment Corporation claims is the largest Web index. According to Alta Vista, the user can search billions of words found in millions of Web pages. In addition, you can access a full-text index of more than 13,000 newsgroups.

Excite! (**http://www.excite.com**) is very versatile because it tracks down information by searching for concepts, not just keywords. Suppose, for example, that you're interested in material on age discrimination. *Excite!* can find such information even though the source describes the phenomenon (such as bias against older people) without ever using the phrase "age discrimination." *Excite!* also provides you with a percentage of how close it "thinks" it came to providing pertinent information on your concept(s). In addition, *Excite!* has such capabilities as finding a specific news article from newsgroups by a text search.

InfoSeek Guide (**http://guide.infoseek.com**) is a search/browse service that returns both search hits and a list of topics related to your search. With each search, you get the most relevant matches, related topics to explore, and current news and views from popular magazines, TV networks, and online experts. *InfoSeek Guide* also helps you find e-mail addresses, stock quotes, company profiles, and other materials.

A frequently-used search engine is *Lycos* (**http://www.lycos.com**). It's simple to operate but, as with any search tool, it takes practice and patience to master. Take the time now to connect to *Lycos*, and we'll take it for a test run. The instructions on the opening page will tell you almost everything you need to know. To search, enter a word into the white text entry box and press the submit button. *Lycos* will refer back to its database of information and return a page of hyperlinked resources containing the word you entered. When the query results come back to you, notice that they are hyperlinks to various sites on the Internet.

Regardless of which search engine you use, remember that they are all fast but dumb. In the spina bifida topic, for example, you'll get hundreds of "hits" that are probably not appropriate for your research paper or class presentation. To perform an effective search, you will need to spend time before the search preparing a search strategy. When you do research using an automated tool like a search engine, you can expect many links to be unrelated to your topic. Continuous research in advanced computing will undoubtedly result in smarter search engines. Until then, the most intelligent researcher is at the keyboard. Despite some misses, you'll find that search engines are very powerful tools and will save you time in the long run.

One last comment on search engines: these tools don't directly search the Internet. They actually search a database that is derived from the Internet. Here is how it works. Initially, information robots (automated programming tools) sift and categorize information on the Internet and place it into a database. It is this database that is inspected when you use a search engine. Therefore, each search engine is only as effective as its cadre of robots that generate the database. Thus it is wise not to rely on just one search engine. Use several, because what one does not find, another might.

Here's a way to test the skills you've developed from your accumulated Internet experience. Using *Yahoo!* and *Lycos* (or any of the other search tools described in this chapter) find information on the Web related to the words given below. Compare the results with searches using the additional resources provided at the bottom of this box. The last three resources (MetaCrawler, FindSpot, and Search.com) allow you to choose from a collection of search tools.

Assimilation	Cohort
Culture	Minority
Stratification	Ageism

WebCrawler
  http://www.webcrawler.com

BigFoot
  http://www.bigfoot.com

HotBot
  http://www.hotbot.com

Dogpile.com
  http://www.dogpile.com

MetaCrawler
  http://www.metacrawler.com

Findspot
  http://www.findspot.com

Search.com
  http://www.search.com

Activity:
The Great Cybertrip

Obtaining information on the Web is easy. It may be somewhat harder to find the *right* information, however. Discovering the correct information is still exciting and interesting, not unlike getting lost and finding your way again in an unfamiliar city. The first list is a set of some commonly-heard terms in psychology. See what you can find on these topics. How have each of these terms enhanced our understanding of our society?

- Latchkey Children
- Magnetic Resonance Imaging
- Sexual Harassment
- REM Sleep
- Intelligence Testing

- Psychotropic Drugs
- Fetal Alcohol Syndrome
- Gestalt Therapy
- Open Adoption
- Date Rape

Understanding psychology often means learning about the women and men who have made significant contributions in both theory and methodology. Below is a short list of some pioneering thinkers from the nineteenth and twentieth centuries. Some of them will be very easy to track down while other will not. We hope you'll find both their perspectives and their lives interesting.

Your assignment, should you accept it, is to put together a brief history of the psychologists listed below and their important contributions. If you want more of a challenge, suggest four substitutions and explain the reasons for your choices.

- Sigmund Freud
- Carl Jung
- Mary Clover Jones
- Robert Sternberg
- Elizabeth Loftus
- Hermann Rorschach
- J. B. Watson
- Jean Piaget
- Carol Gilligan

- Fritz Perls
- Albert Bandura
- Abraham Maslow
- Karen Horney
- B. F. Skinner
- Anna Freud
- Erik Erikson
- Carl Rogers
- William James

Remember to use all of the resources at your disposal. Begin with *Yahoo!* and then move to the other search engines. Check the obscure as well as the popular resources. You are also welcome to read ahead to Chapter 3, which explains how to use e-mail and newsgroups. These resources may be helpful, too.

Chapter 3
Traveling in Style
As You Like It

We shape our tools and afterwards our tools shape us.

By now you have probably wandered through some of the many resources offered on the Web. In this chapter we will cover additional techniques to make your Web experience more enjoyable and beneficial.

Section 3.1
Coffee, tea, or milk?—Customizing

On the Internet, saving time is critical if you have to use a modem and an Internet Service Provider (ISP) to cruise the Net. If you know what your browser can and cannot do, and if you configure the options for your browser so that it is most efficient for you, you will save both time and money. Try the modifications described below as you read; also, feel free to jump to the information that is most important to you.

Some of you may want a more detailed description of your Netscape browser. Netscape has included access to a detailed set of descriptions and instructions on its homepage. To access the Netscape *Navigator Handbook*, select *Help* from the menu bar and choose *Handbook* from the menu list. This will connect you to Netscape's online handbook. Because this information is online and not held within your browser, you need an active Internet connection to use it. You can access this same information from the following URL:

http://home.netscape.com/eng/mozilla/3.0/handbook/

For information on how to get the most out of *Internet Explorer* go to the following URL:

http://www.clubie.com

The site offers information on *Explorer* features and updates, Frequently Asked Questions (FAQs), and Tips and Tricks.

Setting Options

You have several ways to customize the appearance and behavior of your browser. These customizing features are known as *Preferences* or *Options*. Descriptions for some of the *Preferences/Options* follow, as well as the reasons you might want to change them. After you investigate *Preferences/Options*, you'll be able to explore the other custom features on your own.

Navigator

Navigator lists common functions under the *Edit/Preferences* menu on the menu bar at the top of the browser window. Select *Edit* and a pop-up window will appear (Figure 3.1). Once you've selected *Preferences*, you'll notice that the preferences are broken down into categories according to function. The different categories are listed in the left pane of the window (Figure 3.2). Each category has a plus sign (+) next to it;

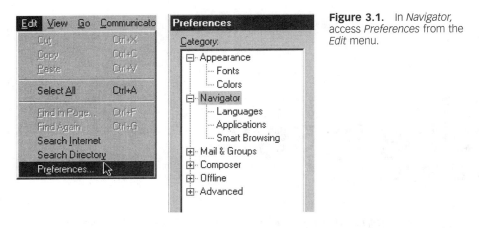

Figure 3.1. In *Navigator*, access *Preferences* from the *Edit* menu.

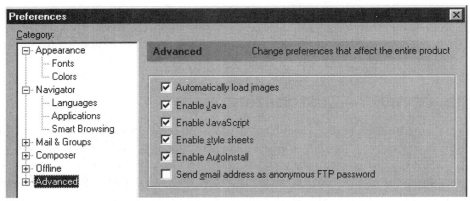

Figure 3.2. From *Navigator's Preferences* menu, you can select options to customize your browser.

clicking the plus sign will expand or collapse the submenu for that category. Notice that there are check marks by some of the options. Look at *Advanced/Auto Load Images*, for example. When there is a check mark, images will be loaded automatically. If you select this option again, the check mark disappears and subsequently pages will load the text without the time-consuming images. Give it a try. Additional preferences can be accessed from the other *Preferences* sub-menus.

Explorer

Internet Explorer lists common functions under the *View/Internet Options* menu (Figure 3.3). Select *Internet Options* from the *View* menu and a pop-up window will appear (Figure 3.4). You'll notice that the options are broken down into tabbed pages. Clicking on a tab will take you to the page for that category of options. Although each tabbed page is different from the next, there are instructions to guide you through the steps. For example, click on the *Advanced* tab and scroll down to *Show Pictures*. When there is a check mark, images will be loaded automatically. Without a check mark, pages will load the text without the time-consuming images. Additional options can be accessed from the other tabs.

Now that you know where to go to modify the setup for your browser, we'll describe some of the features you may want to modify. You will probably want to look at each preference even if you choose not to modify it. Also, keep in mind that some of these changes are not relevant to your setup; others require specific information in order for your browser to work with your ISP. You can always check the online *Navigator Handbook* for help.

Homepage

You might want to modify the location of your homepage. A homepage is like "home" in a game of hopscotch. It is the place you begin hopping from square to square. If you're working with a browser that hasn't been customized before, the company that made the browser probably chose the homepage. If you're work-

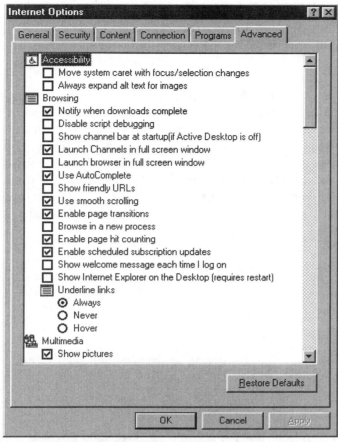

Figure 3.4. In *Explorer,* you can customize your browser from the *Internet Options* menu.

ing on one of your school's computers, then the homepage may already be set to the school's page. If you're permitted to change the homepage, then decide what you want to designate as your homepage. By now you've probably found something on the Web that you are willing to call home. When *your* homepage is properly set, every time you start your browser or select *Home* from the toolbar, you'll end up at this place.

Navigator

Open the *Edit/Preferences* menu and choose *Navigator.* To the right of the window you will see a dialog box within the *Home page* control panel (Figure 3.5) that allows you to set your homepage. Type in the URL of your new homepage.

Figure 3.3. In *Explorer,* access *Internet Options* from the *View* menu.

Explorer

Open the *View/Internet Options* menu. Choose the *General* tab, where you will find a place to type in the address of your Home URL (Figure 3.6).

Linkage

You have probably noticed that hyperlinks are normally blue (unless someone has changed the default color). Once you've accessed the page that the hyperlink represents, it changes to purple. Think of this as the bread crumb principle. The purple links remind you that you've already been down a particular path (link) and that you might want to select a different path. Eventually, however, the hyperlink will change back to its default color. But you can designate the elapsed time before a hyperlink changes back to the default color. You can also choose the default color. Generally, the more time you spend on the Internet, the more quickly (within 24 hours, for example) your links should revert to default. If you travel frequently and find that your hyperlinks are always purple, then your expiration limit may be set too long.

Navigator

From the *Edit/Preferences* menu, open the *Preferences* window and select the *Navigator* category. At the bottom of the window, you will see a *History* dialog box that allows you to set the length of time in days for hyperlinks to expire (Figure 3.7).

Explorer

Open the *View/Internet Options* menu and choose the *General* tab (Figure 3.6). At the bottom of the window, you will see a *History* dialog box that allows you to select the length of time in days for hyperlinks to expire.

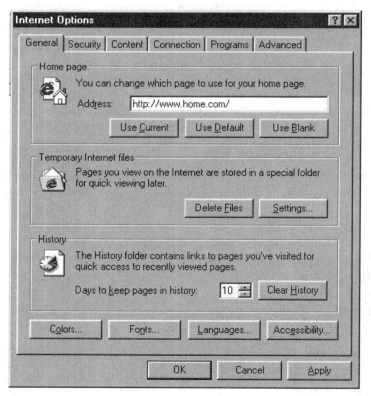

Figure 3.6 Use the *View/Internet Options* menu in *Explorer* to designate a home page.

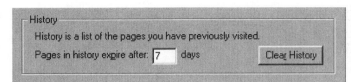

Figure 3.7. In *Navigator,* from the *Edit/Preferences* menu, select the *Navigator* category to access the *History* dialog box. Set the length of time for hyperlinks to expire.

Font Style, Size, and Color

If you spend a great deal of time on the computer, then you realize the importance of adjusting your monitor, desk, and keyboard to minimize potential eye strain and muscle fatigue. Selecting a font of appropriate color, style, and size should help alleviate the hazard.

Navigator

To change the default style and size of the font, select the *Edit/Preferences* menu. Select the *Appearance/ Font* category from this window. You may modify the default settings for both the font size and style used by your browser.

To view other possible font settings, select the appropriate *Font* pull-down menu (Figure 3.8). You should work primarily with the variable width font setting because it is used for the normal text on your browser. (Fixed width fonts are generally used when a page designer is illustrating computer code or text requiring uniform spacing.) In the *Font* pull-down menus you can select from numerous font styles and sizes. When you click the OK button, those font settings will be selected as the default for your browser. If you like your selection, click the OK button at the bottom of the *Fonts* window.

To change the default colors, select the *Edit/Preferences* menu. Select the *Appearance/Colors* category from this window. You may modify the default color settings used by your browser for the hyperlinks (*Unvisited Links* and *Visited Links*) and regular text containing no hyperlinks (*Text*) (Figure 3.9).

To change the color setting, select the appropriate color button. A small window will appear displaying numerous color choices. Click on a color. If you like your choice, click the OK button in the *Colors* window.

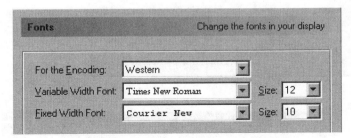

Figure 3.8. In *Navigator,* use the *Fonts* pull-down menus to select font styles and sizes.

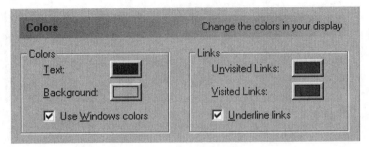

Figure 3.9. In *Navigator,* to change the color setting click on the appropriate color button. Then click on a color in the color choices that are displayed.

Experiment with the *Colors* window. Try to modify both the text and background colors. Remember not to go overboard with your power; you still need to be able to read the words on the page. Some font colors or sizes may be difficult to read and may cause eye strain.

Explorer

Internet Explorer allows you to change font settings by opening the *View/Internet Options* menu. Choose the *General* tab and then click on the *Fonts* button. Once there, you can change fonts depending on what is loaded into your computer (Figure 3.10). Some web sites offer versions of their site in different languages. If you need to change the *language*, follow the same process as you would to change *fonts* but this time click on the *Language* button to view and change what *languages* you may have loaded onto your computer. By clicking on the *Colors* button you may modify the default color settings for the hyperlinks and regular text. In the *Colors* box (Figure 3.11), select the appropriate color button. A small window will appear displaying color choices; click on a color and then click the OK button (Figure 3.12).

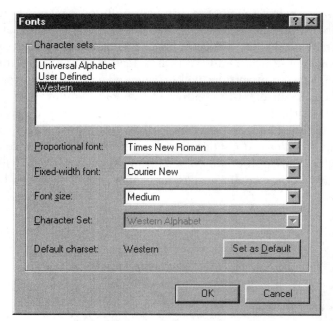

Figure 3.10. To change the font selection in *Explorer*, open the *View/Internet Options* menu, choose the *General* tab, and then click on the *Fonts* button.

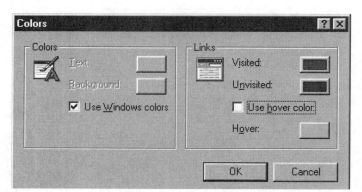

Figure 3.11. To change the color selection in *Explorer*, open the *View/Internet Options* menu, choose the *General* tab, and then click on the *Colors* button.

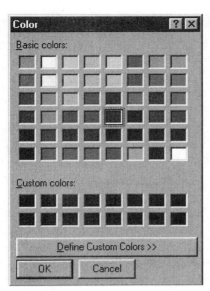

Figure 3.12. Click on a color and then click the OK button.

Although we have not discussed all of the options, you probably have enough information to understand how to use them. Experiment with the settings on your own. You can always check the online *Navigator Handbook* . If you are using *Explorer* and need more help, go to the *Help* menu and select *Contents and Index*. The pop-up window contains a list of topics with more information on each.

Section 3.2
Wish you were here—Communicating

Navigator and most other browsers allow you to communicate through e-mail, newsgroups, and online interest groups. E-mail links are built into many Web pages and enable you to send correspondence directly to other people through the Internet.

E-mail

E-mail is the electronic exchange of mail among people. This exchange is from one person to one (or more) specified people. Like Web browsers and Web servers, e-mail operates according to a Client-Server model. Your client software asks a server computer for mail addressed to you. Your mail server is operated and maintained by the administrator of your campus or ISP. Although your Web server speaks a computer protocol called HyperText Transport Protocol (HTTP), your mail server speaks a computer protocol called Simple Mail Transport Protocol (SMTP).

Think of the server as your mailbox. The mailbox is where mail addressed to you is stored until you pick it up. You use your mail client to retrieve your mail from your mailbox.

Gaining access to an e-mail server is easy. If you are at a campus that has provided you with Internet access, you should be able to apply for an e-mail account through your campus computer administrator. Otherwise, you can apply for an e-mail account through an ISP. If you use an ISP to access the Internet, you probably have e-mail capabilities. In order to properly configure your browser for sending e-mail, you need to know (1) your e-mail address and (2) the name of your mail server.

Before configuring the browser for e-mail, let's look at the form of an e-mail address: NAME@HOST.DOMAIN. It is not necessary to have a full name for the NAME part of the address; in fact, some addresses use only numbers.

The @ symbol in e-mail addresses is known simply as the "at" symbol. Around the world, it is known by more colorful names. For example, in Italy and in France it is known as "chiocciolina" and "petit escargot" (little snail); in the Netherlands it's api (short for apestaart, monkey's tail); in Norway it's "kariel-bolle" (a twisted cinnamon bun); in Denmark it's "snabel A" (an A with a trunk); in Germany it's "Klammeraffe" (spider monkey); and in Finland it's called "miau" (for another animal with a tail).

Here is a typical e-mail address.

plattjeff@niacc.cc.ia.us

The three basic components of an e-mail address include

user name	platjeff
host server	niacc
domain	cc.ia.us

Send a note if you have any comments about this manual.

Your *User Name* is also the NAME associated with your e-mail address. The @ symbol always follows the NAME and then the name of the server computer (HOST). The domain in the e-mail format, just like the domain of the URL format, is used to indicate the affiliation of the user. Notice that there are no spaces anywhere in an e-mail address. Sometimes dashes, periods, or underscores are used as separators in e-mail addresses. Also, e-mail addresses are not case sensitive, so you can capitalize letters or not at your discretion.

Your campus computer administrator or your ISP will provide you with an e-mail address. This is the address you'll give to your friends. It will also be posted with any correspondence you send on the Internet.

Communicator

Configuring *Communicator*, part of your Netscape package along with *Navigator*, to send and receive e-mail only takes two steps:

First: Netscape *Communicator* includes an e-mail and newsgroup reading program called Netscape *Messenger*. To set your personal information, select the *Edit/Preferences* menu and open the *Mail and Newsgroups* window. Select the *Identity* category and you will see the text entry boxes where you can enter your information (Figure 3.13).

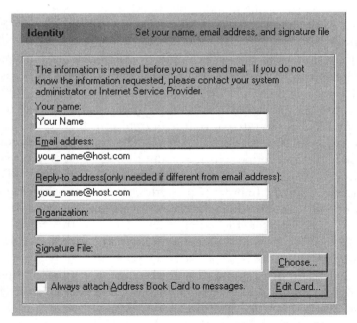

Figure 3.13. Configure Netscape *Communicator* to *send* e-mail by entering your personal information in the *Identity* screen. The *Signature* feature can be used to place standard information (such as your address and phone number) at the bottom of your messages.

90

Second: To set your e-mail information, select the *Edit/Preferences* menu and open the *Mail and Newsgroups* window. Select the *Servers* category and you will see the text entry boxes (Figure 3.14). After you've entered the correct information, restart the browser program. Now you should have the ability to send and receive e-mail. Think about it! You'll save on postage and long-distance phone bills.

Now let's send some e-mail. Select the *Communicator* option from the menu bar and choose *Messenger*. A new window will open (Figure 3.15).

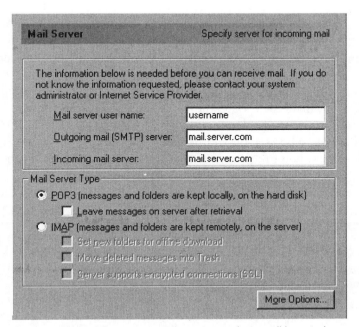

Figure 3.14. Configure *Communicator* to *receive* e-mail by entering server information on the *Mail Server* screen.

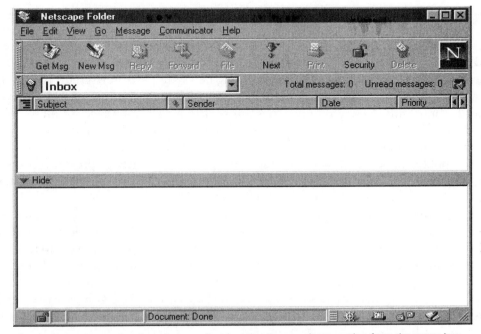

Figure 3.15. To send and receive e-mail, select the *Communicator* option from the menu bar and choose *Messenger*. The window that opens is similar to a Web browser.

Notice that this window is similar to a Web browser. (It is also similar to the news reader that we will discuss later.) To view your mail, select the *Get Msg* button. If you have mail, then it will appear in the top frame of the window. All incoming mail arrives in the *Inbox*. When you select the *Inbox* in the pull-down menu, its contents will appear in the top frame of the window. When you select a specific mail item in the top frame, you will see the contents displayed at the bottom of the window. To test the setup, send yourself an e-mail message. Next, write your congressperson. You can find his/her address in the box below.

Explorer

Choose the *View/Internet Options* menu, click on the *Programs* tab and then choose the *Mail* menu. From there you are allowed to select whatever "e-mail programs" you have loaded onto your computer. You fill out your exact e-mail information within your e-mail program, not within Explorer.

Most e-mail systems use a single machine to handle both incoming and outgoing mail. However, some systems use a different machine for incoming and outgoing mail. In Figure 3.14, note that two different text entry boxes are provided for the mail server. If your system uses just one machine, enter the mail server twice. The person who sets up your account should be able to give you all the information you need. If they are less than helpful, then it is generally safe to assume that the address for both your incoming and outgoing mail server is MAIL.HOST.DOMAIN.

Now that you've got the basics down, here are three sites you'll find useful.

A Beginner's Guide to Effective Email
http://www.webfoot.com/advice/email.top.html

The Electronic Activist
http://www.ifas.org/activist/index.html

Congressional E-mail Directory
http://www.webslingerz.com/jhoffman/congress-email.html

Newsgroups

Many browsers enable users to exchange ideas by using newsgroups. A newsgroup is a group of people who participate in a specialized discussion on the Internet. These groups are open forums in which all are welcomed to contribute. Newsgroup postings are sent to a common place for all to read and reply. Some are moderated by one or more people who post items for discussion and referee any electronic brawls that may ensue. However, not all newsgroups are rife with disagreement. Many offer excellent opportunities for polite conversation with courteous people. All newsgroups provide a place where people can bring new ideas and perspectives to the screen. If e-mail is like the postal service, though, newsgroups are like coffee houses on open microphone night.

What is the purpose of the newsgroups if people just contribute ideas and comments on a particular subject? Newsgroups are places where you can ask questions, get ideas, and learn about specific topics. Select a group that has an interest common to yours or a topic that you are trying to learn about. You'll find that there are many newsgroups that focus on psychology and psychology-related areas.

The names of newsgroups usually describe their discussion topic. There are several major newsgroup categories. The ones you'll probably use most are the SCI and ALT groups. We've included a list of relevant newsgroups in Appendix I. You'll find some of them interesting and helpful as a supplement to your studies in Psychology.

Here is a typical newsgroup URL. Newsgroup names are divided into several descriptive words separated by a period and organized according to a hierarchy. Note that newsgroup URLs don't use the double slash (//).

news:sci.psychology.consciousness

Here are the main components:

protocol	news:
top category	sci
sub category	psychology
sub category	consciousness

To configure your browser to connect to a newsgroup, you will need the name of the server computer that handles newsgroups. (Get this from the same people who gave you your mail-server address.) You'll perform almost the same procedure you used to set up your e-mail service.

Communicator

To set your newsgroup information, select the *Edit/Preferences* menu and open the *Mail & Groups* window. Select the *Groups Server* tab and you will see the text entry boxes (Figure 3.16). Once you enter the correct information and restart the browser program, you should be able to view newsgroups. You may find that you can't access some newsgroups. Check to make sure your ISP subscribes to these groups. If not, your ISP will usually do so if you make a request.

You should now be ready for an adventure. When you use *Navigator* to read or post articles to newsgroups, you won't be using the same window that you used for browsing the Web. For newsgroups, you'll use what is typically called a *news reader*. To start your news reader, select the *Communicator* option from the menu bar and choose *Messenger* or *Collabra*, depending on your version of *Communicator*. A new window will open (Figure 3.17).

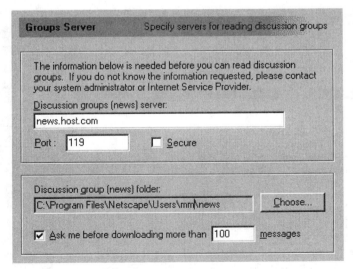

Figure 3.16. Enter server information in *Communicator's Groups Server* window to configure your browser to read newsgroups.

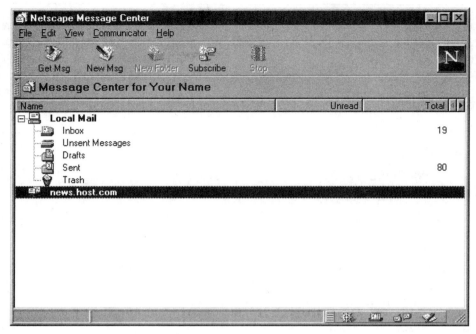

Figure 3.17. *Navigator* includes a built-in news reader. Its feature are similar to both the mail client and the Web browser.

Note how this window resembles the Web browser, as well as how it differs. To view a larger list of newsgroups you can select *File/Subscribe to Discussion Groups* from the menu bar. A new window will open with tabs to view *All Groups, Search* newsgroups, and view *New* newsgroups that may have been added since you last logged on (Figure 3.18). Select *All Groups*. A large list of newsgroups will appear on the left.

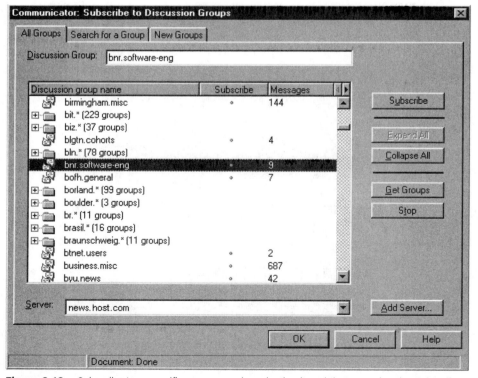

Figure 3.18. Subscribe to a specific newsgroup by selecting it and then pressing the *Subscribe* button; then click OK.

You can subscribe to a specific one by selecting it and then pressing the *Subscribe* button on the right; then click OK. When you are done, close this window and return to the *Messenger* or *Collabra* window. In *Collabra*, you'll immediately see the newsgroups to which you subscribed, and you will be able to read each newsgroup or article by clicking on it. In *Messenger*, you'll have to select your news server from the pull-down menu (the same pull-down where you selected your Inbox). When you select a newsgroup, the individual articles will appear in the top frame of the window. Finally, when you select a specific article, you'll see the contents displayed at the bottom of the news reader window. Now, take some time and explore.

Explorer

Choose the *View/Internet Options* menu. Click on the *Programs* tab and then choose the *News* menu. From there you are allowed to choose whatever "news programs" you have loaded onto your computer. You fill out your *News* information within your *News* program, not within *Explorer*.

News servers use a protocol called *NetNews Transfer Protocol*, or *NNTP*. You might need to ask around to find out the address for your news server. If you can't find someone to help, you can probably assume that the address for your news server is NEWS.HOST.DOMAIN.

The only way to really understand what newsgroups are like is to try them. Here are a several news-groups that will get you started. Connect to one of interest and read some of the postings. For your first time, you should just read the postings and follow some of the conversations. (This is called lurking.) Connections or threads develop between postings as people add comments to earlier postings. As you become familiar with the topic of discussion, you might post a comment yourself. Before you jump in, you may want to read the section titled "Language for the Road" in this chapter.

news:sci.psychology

news:sci.psychology.journals.psyche

news: sci.psychology.theory

news:alt.psychology.help

news:alt.psychology.personality

Two useful tools for newsgroups are *DejaNews* and *Reference.COM*. *DejaNews* (**http://www.dejanews.com/**) allows you to search for topics in newsgroups. *Reference.COM* (**http://www.reference.com/**) notifies you by e-mail if topics specified by you are discussed. Take a look at both of these!

Chat

This is yet another avenue for communication. It is probably the one you'll choose if you like to talk. Unlike e-mail and newsgroups, which require you to wait for a response, chat rooms are real-time. This means that you are conversing and observing conversations as they happen. As with newsgroups, it is best to observe the interactions of several chat rooms and read the new user information before you jump in. Some rooms can be excessive and vulgar, but many are frequented by polite people with a genuine desire for conversation. Just like newsgroups, chat rooms are organized by topic and you can usually anticipate the discussion by the name of the group. Unlike newsgroups, there are few academic-specific chat rooms; therefore, you'll probably find that they are a great place for general conversation.

Just to get you started, here are a few Web-based chat groups. Read the instructions and ask for help if you need it.

Jammin's ChatPlanet Chat Room!
http://www.jammin.com/livechat.html

MSNBC Chat
http://msnbc.com/chat/default.asp

Quicken Chat
http://quicken.excite.com/forums/

Unlike e-mail and newsgroups, you will be frequently asked to login or register before beginning to chat. Often you'll even be given a password. Always, read the rules for participating and ask for help if you don't understand something. The participants are generally very helpful. The other characteristic of chat rooms is that typically you will use a "handle" or pseudonym when you post a message.

Language for the Road

A few words of caution. Unlike normal conversations between people, electronic exchanges don't convey vocal inflections, facial expression, and body language. (These things aren't easily digitized and transmitted across a copper wire. To be sure, there are such things as Internet telephones and video conferencing, but for most of us they are not affordable and practical.) You will need to practice the way you communicate electronically and be patient when someone misinterprets something you've "said." For example, suppose you tell a joke. Because the reader only gets the text, she may think that you are serious and take offense. Computer people learned about this problem a long time ago and an innovative solution has been developed. The solution is a collection of "smileys."

Here are some smileys; tilt your head to the left to interpret them:

:-)	smile	:-x	my lips are sealed
;-)	wink	:-o	oh!
:- (	sad	:-I	indifferent
:-[	very sad	:-*	kiss

Because you will eventually get tired of typing all of the things you want to say, several acronyms are in common use. Here are a few:

BTW	By The Way
IMHO	In My Humble Opinion
FYI	For Your Information
FWIW	For What It's Worth
TIA	Thanks in Advance
ADN	Any Day Now
B4N	Bye For Now

Now for a couple of terms. Like any other culture, the Internet community has borrowed some common words to describe special situations. Here are two that you'll see:

Flame This refers to the act of yelling, insulting, or degrading a person or his or her character. You can expect to get flamed if you don't follow certain basic rules of netiquette (etiquette of the Net).

Spam This refers to the act of posting a comment, message, or advertisement to multiple newsgroups when the note doesn't really pertain to the newsgroup topic. It is the Internet equivalent of sending junk mail.

Here are a couple of Web resources that you will want to read when you begin communicating online. They are very helpful and entertaining. Enjoy!

E-Mail Etiquette
http://www.iwillfollow.com/email.htm

Electronic Frontier Foundation's Unofficial Smiley Dictionary
http://www.eff.org/papers/eegtti/eeg_286.html

Section 3.3
The fun is in the going—Extending

In early Web history, travel was pretty basic. The browser was a piece of software that acted as a totally self-contained vehicle. When you hooked it up, it contained everything you needed to cruise the Net. This has changed. As the Web grows larger, people develop new formats of information they wish to include on the Web. These new formats allow for a richer expression. Things like digital video, audio, animations, interactive games, and 3D worlds are currently very common on the Internet. As people demand more functionality from the Internet, new formats will become available. To cope with this continuing change, Netscape and *Explorer* developed a way to add functionality without overloading the basic browser design.

Helpers and Plug-ins

Early Web pages included only text and images. They were much like brochures with the ability to hyperlink to other pages. The images that were included in Web pages were in a GIF format. However, to accommodate new image formats like JPEG, browsers turned to helper applications. If a page designer included a JPEG image, then an external helper application program displayed the image for viewing outside of the browser. Rather than having to rely on external programs, plug-in programs were developed to add the same features within the browser itself. For example, if you want to listen to music across the Internet from your browser, then you could install a plug-in that allows the browser to understand the audio format.

Netscape and *Explorer* have developed many plug-ins, and they are still the place to turn when you want one. An important thing, though: adding plug-ins to your browser will increase your memory (RAM) requirements. If you add too many plug-ins, your browser might stop working. Only install the plug-ins that you're going to use regularly.

These addresses will take you to the place where you can download the plug-ins to your computer. The developers also provide a very good description of how to install and use the plug-ins.

RealAudio by Progressive Networks
http://www.real.com/products/player/index.html

Shockwave by MacroMedia
http://www.macromedia.com/shockwave/download/

Java and JavaScript

Grab a cup of coffee for this one. Helper application programs (helpers) and plug-ins weren't enough to satisfy Web developers. Web developers wanted even more—*more* flexibility, *more* interactivity, and *more* control. *Java* and *JavaScript* were developed to provide the more that developers wanted. But to understand what Java and JavaScript are, you need to understand what Web pages *were not*. Web page designers didn't claim to *program* Web pages; rather, they said that they *wrote*, *designed*, or *created* Web pages. You may wonder what the difference is. Programming is the process of developing a set of instructions that perform a specific function. Writing, designing, and creating are activities that communicate ideas. When executed, programs actively do things, whereas Web pages communicate ideas (by bringing together different media).

One type of media, interactive programs, did not exist in Web pages until the programming languages *Java* and *JavaScript* were made available. Now, besides communicating ideas, Web pages can also interactively do things as well. They add functionality to Web pages just as helpers and plug-ins do, but they provide much greater flexibility. The fundamental difference between the two languages is that *JavaScript* is usually integrated with the Web page and runs on the client side, whereas *Java* is usually integrated on the server side. The results are probably best understood by examining a few *Java* and *JavaScript* programs for yourself. If you are using Netscape *Navigator 2.0* or greater (or Microsoft *Internet Explorer 3.0* or greater), then you have the ability to view and interact with these programs, although the 4.0 versions do a much better job at handling all flavors of Javascript. But a word of caution here, not all Javascript is created equal. Do not be surprised if a web page appears and functions correctly in *Navigator* and then fails to appear or work correctly while being viewed in *Explorer*, or vice versa. This can happen for a variety of reasons but it most often occurs when Javascripting is involved. Most quality sites will take the differences of the two browsers into account but even then some strange things can and do happen.

There are two other developments in web creation that should also be mentioned: Cascading style sheets and dynamic HTML. Cascading style sheets are a major improvement in Web development because they allow Web designers to control the style and layout of multiple Web pages all at once. Cascading style sheets work like templates. Web developers define a style for an HTML element and then apply it to as many Web pages as they need. Utilizing CSS, when you want to make a change, you change the style, and that element is updated automatically wherever it appears within the site, where-as before CSS each element would have to be individually updated. *Navigator 4.0* and *Explorer 4.0* both support cascading style sheets.

Dynamic HTML is a combination of HTML, scripting (mostly Javascripting), and CSS that helps create robust, interactive Web pages without increasing the download times for these pages to be viewed. The standards for dynamic HTML are still being hammered out and *Navigator* and *Explorer* are handling it in different ways, so expect differences.

http://www.stars.com/Authoring/Style/Sheets/

http://www.htmlhelp.com/reference/css/

If you want to see Dynamic HTML in action go to Macromedia's Dynamic HTML Zone at **http://www.dhtmlzone.com/alt.html.** Remember that you must have a 4.0 version of *Navigator* or *Explorer* to view much of this.

Activity:
A Talkabout Tour

Learning doesn't stop when you leave the classroom or laboratory. The people around you, textbooks, libraries, and the Internet are all important resources that broaden your education. In particular, the Web, newsgroups, chat rooms, and e-mail can all help you become well-rounded and well-connected.

E-mail
Because you have a wealth of information at your fingertips, take the time to get some e-mail addresses from your instructor or other students. Most good e-mail software will provide you with a mechanism to store these addresses for easy retrieval. Begin exchanging e-mail with some of these people and you'll find that there is plenty of help available when you need it.

Newsgroups
Make it a practice to browse newsgroups. Plenty are of general interest; you should also make a habit of checking into a newsgroup that focuses on important topics discussed in class. By visiting many different newsgroups, you'll always have the latest scoop in a variety of subjects.

Chat
Chat rooms may or may not enhance your education. However, you might be able to find a chat room that is relatively empty. If so, arrange a fixed weekly time when you and your classmates can get together to work out problems or discuss material covered that week. A better option is to meet in person, but if this is impossible, chat rooms can provide an alternative.

Web Page
If you are using an ISP for Internet access, then you probably have access to posting information on your homepage. Consider using it as a way to bring other students together for discussion. Check with your instructor and you may find that he or she is willing to help you with this activity.

Appendix I
Internet Resources for Psychology

A hot medium is one that extends the single sense in "high definition."
High definition is the state of being filled with data.

Here are a number of links that you should find "ve-e-ry interesting." Think of this as a starter kit for further investigation. It includes websites for using the Internet, digital library websites, and general websites for the Humanities and Social Sciences. Sites are provided for Psychology and useful Psychology-related sites, followed by some examples of Psychology newsgroups.

We'd like to get faculty and student input on improving the Psychology and Psychology-related sites. What sites should be included in the future that students have found especially useful? Which URLs are the least informative? Please send all suggestions to **plattjef@niacc.cc.ia.us**.

Several comments are in order before you begin surfing. First, don't be discouraged if your first try to link to a site produces a message like "Unable to connect to remote host." The rule of thumb is to try the same site three times in a row before proceeding to another URL. (Remember, you're still trying to communicate with the World Wide Wait.) Second, be careful typing site locations. If you mistype one character (capital letters matter), the address won't work. Third, Web sites come and go more often than print media. What is on the Internet today may be gone tomorrow. Fourth, a tilde (~) usually designates a site maintained by a person, rather than an organization or some "non-person." These are the sites most likely to disappear on the Web. Finally, we list just a few newsgroups. If you are an archaeologist (or anyone who has done some digging), there are more newsgroups than you could possibly dream of excavating. Try **http://www.tile.net/tile/news/** to unearth your favorite newsgroup. Get down!

Websites for Using the Internet

Internet Starter Kit (Macmillan Computer Publishing)
http://www.mcp.com/resources/geninternet/

Web Resources
http://www.w3.org

World Wide Web FAQ
http://sunsite.unc.edu/boutell/faq/faq.txt

Learn the Net
http://www.learnthenet.com/english/index.html

Understanding and Using the Internet
http://www2.pbs.org/uti/

Newbie Training
http://www.newbie.net/CyberCourse

The Internet for Social Scientists
http://www.unesco.org/most/brochur3.htm

Interactive Guide to the Internet
http://www.sierramm.com/smpnet.html

Evaluating Internet Resources
http://www.albany.edu/library/internet/evaluate.html

Evaluating Quality on the Net
http://www.tiac.net/users/hope/findqual.html

Digital Library Websites

Gateway to Europe's National Libraries
http://portico.bl.uk/gabriel/

Worldwide Digital Library Research Projects
http://www.dlib.org/projects.html#national

Digital Library Initiative (Social Science Team)
http://anshar.grainger.uiuc.edu/dlisoc/socsci_site/index.html

University of California at Berkeley
http://elib.cs.berkeley.edu/

University of Michigan
http://www.si.umich.edu/UMDL

University of Illinois
http://dli.grainger.uiuc.edu

University of California at Santa Barbara
http://alexandria.sdc.ucsb.edu/

Carnegie Mellon University
http://www.informedia.cs.cmu.edu

Library of Congress Digital Library
http://www.loc.gov/

Berkeley Digital Library SunSITE
http://sunsite.berkeley.edu/

Humanities Texts
http://english-server.hss.cmu.edu

eLib Homepage
http://ukoln.bath.ac.uk/elib/

The Electric Library
http://www.elibrary.com/

The Electronic Newsstand
http://www.enews.com

General Websites for Humanities and Social Sciences

The HUMBUL Gateway: International Resources for the Humanities
http://users.ox.ac.uk/~humbul/

Humanities HUB: Selected Resources for the Social Sciences
and Humanities
http://www.gu.edu.au/gwis/hub/

TradeWave Galaxy: Humanities/Social Sciences Indices
http://www.einet.net

Social Science Indices
http://www.osu.edu/units/sociology/indices.htm

Coombsweb Social Sciences Server
http://coombs.anu.edu.au/

INFOMINE for the Social Sciences, Humanities, and the Arts
http://lib-www.ucr.edu/liberal/

The Argus Clearinghouse: Arts and Humanities/Social Sciences
and Social Issues
http://www.clearinghouse.net/index.html

The WWW Virtual Library
http://vlib.stanford.edu/Overview.html

Voice of the Shuttle Guide to the Humanities and Social Sciences
http://humanitas.ucsb.edu/

H-Net: Humanities and Social Sciences Online Home Page
http://h-net.msu.edu/

Social Science Information Gateway
http://sosig.ac.uk/

Forum on Technology, Media and Society
http://tunisia.sdc.ucsb.edu/speed/

General Psychology Websites

Getting You Started on Your Career Path!
http://www.umanitoba.ca/counselling/careers.html

Fields of Psychology
http://www.msubillings.edu/PSYCHOLOGY/fields.htm

Psychology.Com created to help people enhance their personal & professional lives
http://www.psychology.com/

Psychology Graduate Schools, Journals, And More
http://pegasus.cc.ucf.edu/~md60207/

Psychology of Invention
http://hawaii.cogsci.uiuc.edu/invent/invention.html

Mind and Body: Renee Descartes to William James
http://serendip.brynmawr.edu/Mind/Table.html

Web Extension to American Psychological Association Style (WEAPAS)
http://www.beadsland.com/weapas/

Psychweb: Psychology and Mental Health
http://www.psychweb.com

Psycsite
http://stange.simplenet.com/psycsite/index.htm

Psychology Related Resources

Prentice Hall Psychology Homepage
http://www.prenhall.com/~psychmap

The ShrinkTank BBS Web Site
http://www.shrinktank.com/

Cognitive and Psychological Sciences on the Internet
http://dawww.essex.ac.uk/~roehl/PsycIndex/

E-Prime: A Cross-platform Experiment Generator Studio for Computerized Behavioral Research
http://www.pstnet.com/e-prime/e-prime.htm

Psychological Resources
http://alabanza.com/kabacoff/Inter-Links/health/psy/psy.html

CTI Centre for Psychology
http://www.york.ac.uk/inst/ctipsych/

Psychology and Related Sites (PsychLab)
http://quarles.unbc.edu/psyc/psychlab/psych.htm

Psychology Web Archive
http://swix.ch/clan/ks/CPSP1.htm

Psychological Associations

Psychology Organizations on the Web
http://www.wesleyan.edu/spn/psych.htm

The American Psychological Association
http://www.apa.org

American Psychological Society
http://www.hanover.edu/psych/APS/aps.html

The British Psychological Society
http://www.bps.org.uk

Society for Neuroscience
http://www.sfn.org/

The Federation of Behavioral, Psychological, and Cognitive Sciences
http://www.am.org/federation/

Society for the Quantitative Analysis of Behavior
http://www.jsu.edu/depart/psychology/sebac/sqab.html

Cognitive Neuroscience Society
http://www.dartmouth.edu/~cns/

International Society of Political Psychology
http://ispp.org:80/

The Society for Judgment and Decision Making
http://www.sjdm.org:80/sjdm/

Society for Computers in Psychology
http://www.lafayette.edu/allanr/scip.html

Psi Chi
http://www.psichi.org/intro.asp

Psychology Journals

The APA Monitor
http://www.apa.org/monitor

Articles About How to Cite Internet Documents (Psychology Web Archives)
http://swix.ch/clan/ks/CPSP22.htm

American Psychological Association (APA) Journals
http://www.apa.org/journals

Journal of Applied Behavior Analysis
**http://www.envmed.rochester.edu/wwwrap/behavior/
jaba/jabahome.htm**

Journal of the Experimental Analysis of Behavior
**http://www.envmed.rochester.edu/wwwrap/behavior/jeab/
jeabhome.htm**

History of Psychology
http://www.WPI.EDU/~histpsy/

Journal of Cognitive Rehabilitation
http://www.neuroscience.cnter.com/nsp/default.htm

Psycoloquy—Psychology
http://www.cogsci.soton.ac.uk/psycoloquy/

Theory & Psychology Journal
http://www.psych.ucalgary.ca/thpsyc/thpsyc.html

Self-Help & Psychology Magazine
http://www.shpm.com/

Annual Reviews
http://www.AnnualReviews.org/ari/

Psychology Related Laboratories

SouthEastern Behavior Analysis Center
http://jsucc.jsu.edu/psychology/sebac.html

University of Southampton Psychology and Cognitive Sciences Centre
http://cogsci.ecs.soton.ac.uk/~harnad/index.html

University of Texas Neural Nets Research Group
http://www.cs.utexas.edu/users/nn/

University of Texas Qualitative Reasoning Research Group
http://www.cs.utexas.edu/users/qr/

University of Waterloo Computational Epistemology Lab
http://cogsci.uwaterloo.ca/

The Institute for Information Technology: Artificial Intelligence Resources
http://ai.iit.nrc.ca/ai_point.html

Austrian Research Institute for AI
http://www.ai.univie.ac.at/oefai/oefai.html

BYU Neural Networks and Machine Learning
http://synapse.cs.byu.edu/home.html

Cambridge University Applied Psychology Unit
http://www.mrc-apu.cam.ac.uk/

CMU—Center for the Neural Basis of Cognition
http://www.cnbc.cmu.edu/

Edgeworth Laboratory for Quantitative Behavioral Science
http://quarles.unbc.ca/psyc/zumbo/edgeworth3.html

EINet Galaxy Psychology Listing
http://galaxy.tradewave.com/galaxy/Social-Sciences/Psychology.html

University of British Columbia Computational Intelligence Lab
http://www.cs.ubc.ca/nest/lci

University of Calgary Psychology Department
http://www.psych.ucalgary.ca/

University of California at Santa Cruz Perceptual Science Lab
http://mambo.ucsc.edu/index.html

University of Maryland at College Park Lab for Automation Psychology
http://www.lap.umd.edu/

University of Michigan AI Lab
http://krusty.eecs.umich.edu/

University of Pennsylvania Institute for Research in Cognitive Science
http://www.cis.upenn.edu/~ircs/homepage.html

U.S. Universities

Index of Psychology and Related Departments
http://psych.hanover.edu/Krantz/other.html

The University of Memphis Psychology Department
http://www.psyc.memphis.edu/psych.htm

Vanderbilt University Psychology Department
http://www.vanderbilt.edu/AnS/psychology/HomePage.html

Carnegie Mellon University (Psychology)
http://www.psy.cmu.edu/

University of California at Davis Center for Neuroscience
http://neuroscience.ucdavis.edu/

University of California at Irvine Cognitive Science Department
http://www.socsci.uci.edu/cogsci/

UCLA Department of Psychology
http://www.psych.ucla.edu/

U. of California at San Diego Cognitive Sciences Department
http://cogsci.ucsd.edu/

U. of New Mexico Psychology Department
http://www.unm.edu/~psych/psych_unm.html

Brown University Psychology Department
http://www.brown.edu/Departments/Psychology/

University of Minnesota Psychology Department
http://www.psych.umn.edu/

Neurosciences at the University of Washington
http://weber.u.washington.edu/~wcalvin/neuro-uw.html

History of Psychology

The Lifschitz Psychology Museum
http://www.netaxs.com/people/aca3/LPM.HTM

Classics in the History of Psychology
http://www.yorku.ca/dept/psych/classics/

The History of Psychology (University of New Brunswick course with links)
http://www.unb.ca/web/units/psych/likely/psyc4053.htm

Developmental Psychology

Developmental Biology, Education Section
http://sdb.bio.purdue.edu/SDBEduca/EducaToC.html

Feldman DEVELOPMENT ACROSS THE LIFESPAN (contains web links)
http://www.prenhall.com/feldman

Rice CHILD AND ADOLESCENT DEVELOPMENT (contains web links)
http://www.prenhall.com/rice

Teratology Society
http://teratology.org/

The Visible Embryo
http://visembryo.com

The Multi-Dimensional Human Embryo
http://embryo.mc.duke.edu/

Obstetric Ultrasound: A Comprehensive Guide to Ultrasound Scans in Pregnancy
http://home.hkstar.com/~joewoo/

Basic Embryology Review Program
http://www.med.upenn.edu/meded/public/berp/

Fetal Diagnosis and Treatment at Vanderbilt University Medical Center
http://webriver.com/bruner/index.htm

APGAR Scoring for Newborns
http://www.childbirth.org/articles/apgar.html

Research Network on Successful Pathways Through Middle Childhood
http://midchild.soe.umich.edu

APA Division 20: Adult Development & Aging
http://www.iog.wayne.edu/apadiv20/apadiv20.htm

American Academy of Pediatrics Website (AAP)
http://www.aap.org/

National Institute of Child Health and Human Development
http://www.nih.gov/nichd/

National Clearinghouse on Child Abuse and Neglect Information
http://www.calib.com/nccanch/

Birth Psychology
http://www.birthpsychology.com/index.html

Educational Psychology

Internet Resources: Educational Psychology
http://www.lib.muohio.edu/edpsych/internetresources.html#EPR

Discovery Based Learning
http://www.academic.marist.edu/discvryl/

Index of Learning Styles (ILS): A testing instrument
http://www2.ncsu.edu/unity/lockers/users/f/felder/public/
ILSpage.html

The Instant Access Treasure Chest: Information on Learning Disabilities
http://www.fln.vcu.edu/ld/ld.html

Tom Allen's Net Place: Teacher Preparation
http://www.humboldt.edu/~tha1/index.html

Teacher-Developed Earth and Space Science Lessons and Classroom Activities
http://cse.ssl.berkeley.edu/lessons/lessons_teacherdeveloped.html

Teachers.Net-The Teacher Website!
http://teachers.net/

Educational Psychology Interactive: Internet Resources
http://www.valdosta.peachnet.edu:80/~whuitt/psy702/internet.html

SERI: Special Education Resources on the Internet
http://www.hood.edu/seri/serihome.html

Mental Health and Adjustment

A Magic Stream of Mental Health, Self-Help and Emotional Awareness
http://fly.hiwaay.net/~garson/

Self-Help & Psychology Magazine
http://www.cybertowers.com/selfhelp/

National Institute of Mental Health
http://www.nimh.nih.gov/home.htm

PsychScapes WorldWide Inc.
http://www.mental-health.com/psychscapes/

Psych Central: Dr. John Grohol's Mental Health Page
http://www.psychcentral.com/

Psychology Self-Help Resources on the Internet
http://www.psychweb.com/counseli.htm

Addiction Resources
http://www.well.com/user/woa/aodsites.htm

The Divorce Support Page
http://www.divorcesupport.com/index.html

More Internet Mental Health Resources
http://www.mentalhealth.com/

Yet More Internet Mental Health Resources
http://www.med.nyu.edu/Psych/src.psych.html

Freudian Slips Eclectic Mental Health, Etc., Site
http://www.fgi.net/~freud/index.htm

Clinical Psychology Resources
http://www.psychologie.uni-bonn.de/kap/links_20.htm

Behavior Online
http://www.behavior.net

Psychological Disorders

Brain Disorders Network/Disorders Described
http://www.brainnet.org/disorder.htm

Nevid/Rathus/Greene ABNORMAL PSYCHOLOGY 3rd Edition
(contains web links for each chapter)
http://cw.prenhall.com/nevid

the Anxiety Panic internet resource (tAPir)
http://www.algy.com/anxiety/index.html

C.H.A.D.D. Attention Deficit Disorder Information
http://www.chadd.org/

Autism Resources
http://web.syr.edu/~jmwobus/autism/

Pendulum's Bipolar Disorder/Manic-Depression Pages
http://www.pendulum.org/index.htm

Internet Depression Resources List
http://earth.execpc.com/~corbeau/

The Schizophrenia Home Page
http://www.schizophrenia.com/

Psychopharmacology Tips
http://uhs.bsd.uchicago.edu/~bhsiung/tips/tips.html

Lecture Notes for a Course in Abnormal Psychology
http://ub-counseling.buffalo.edu/Abpsy/

Traumatic Brain Injury Resource Guide
http://www.callamer.com:80/~cns/

Sensation and Perception

Vision Science
http://www.visionscience.com

Tutorials in Sensation and Perception
http://psych.hanover.edu/Krantz/sen_tut.html

Serendip
http://serendip.brynmawr.edu/bb/

Prevent Blindness America
http://www.prevent-blindness.org/

Lance Hahn's Retina References
http://retina.anatomy.upenn.edu/~lance/retina/retina.html

Seeing, Hearing, and Smelling the World
http://www.hhmi.org/senses/

The James Randi Educational Foundation
http://www.randi.org/

Social Psychology

Social Psychology Network
http://www.wesleyan.edu/spn/

Social Psychology
http://www.trinity.edu/~mkearl/socpsy.html

Collective Behavior and the Social Psychologies of Social Institutions
http://trinity.edu/~mkearl/socpsy-8.html

Social Cognition Archives and Papers
http://www.psych.purdue.edu/~esmith/scarch.html

Psychology and Statistics

Psychology 3030: Intermediate Statistics
http://www.yorku.ca/dept/psych/lab/psy3030/

Statistics and Statistical Graphics Resources
http://www.math.yorku.ca/SCS/StatResource.html

UCLA Statistics Electronic Publications
http://www.stat.ucla.edu/papers/

Psychology and Human Sexuality

Sinclair Intimacy Institute Sexuality Database
http://www.intimacyinstitute.com/sex_data/index.html

The Kinsey Institute for Research in Sex, Gender, and Reproduction
http://www.indiana.edu/~kinsey/

Gender Reassignment Surgery
http://www.grsmontreal.com/welco.htm

Biological Differences
http://nba19.med.uth.tmc.edu/female_anat/index.html

Neuroscience Sources

Systems Neuroscience
http://weber.u.washington.edu/~chudler/ehc.html

The World-Wide Web Virtual Library: Biosciences
http://golgi.harvard.edu/biopages/

The World-Wide Web Virtual Library: Neuroscience (Biosciences)
http://neuro.med.cornell.edu

Neurosciences on the Internet
http://www.neuroguide.com/

Other Neuroscience Areas of Interest

The Journal of Chemical Neuroanatomy
http://np0011.unimaas.nl/cheneu.html

Neuroanatomy Study Slides
http://www.mcl.tulane.edu/student/1997/kenb/neuroanatomy/readme_neuro.html

Towards the Neuronal Substrate of Visual Consciousness
http://www.klab.caltech.edu/~koch/tuscon-94.html

Nervous System Resources

CMU—Center for Cognitive Brain Imaging
http://coglab.psy.cmu.edu/

Basic Human Anatomy
http://www.indiana.edu/~anat215/a215.htm

Shuffle Brain
http://www.indiana.edu/~pietsch/home.html

Neuroanatomy & Neuropathology on the Internet
http://www.dote.hu/~hegedus

The Human Brain Project—Denmark
http://hendrix.ei.dtu.dk/

Brain Model Tutorial
http://pegasus.cc.ucf.edu/~Brainmd1/brain.html

External View of the Brain
http://rpiwww.mdacc.tmc.edu:89/se/anatomy/brain

Learning Guide for the Human Brain
http://uta.marymt.edu/~psychol/brain.html

The Digital Anatomist Interactive Atlases
http://www9.biostr.washington.edu/da.html

Human Image Dataset
http://www.loni.ucla.edu/data/human/

Center for In Vivo Microscopy
http://wwwcivm.mc.duke.edu./

Evolution of the Human Brain
http://citd.scar.utoronto.ca/ANT3032/Henderson/Table.htm

Serendip
http://serendip.brynmawr.edu/

Biology Education Interactive Web: Human Genetics, Neurophysiology, Immunology, & Webcast
Science Lectures
http://www.hhmi.org/grants/lectures/multimedia/

Virtual Hospital: The Human Brain
http://www.vh.org/Providers/Textbooks/BrainAnatomy/BrainAnatomy.html

Human Anatomy On-line (InnerBody.com)
http://www.innerbody.com/indexbody.html

Neuropsychology Central
http://www.premier.net/~cogito/neuropsy.html

Timmons & Hamilton: Drugs, Brains & Behavior
http://www.rci.rutgers.edu/~lwh/drugs/

Biopsychology Links
http://www.uwsp.edu/acad/psych/tbiopsy.htm

PHYSLINK.HTML
http://www.marymt.edu/~psychol/physio/physlink.html

Histology

HistoWeb
**http://www.kumc.edu/instruction/medicine/anatomy/histoweb/
nervous/nervous.htm**

Histology of the Peripheral Nervous System
http://www.mc.vanderbilt.edu/~alemanma/nerve.html

Psychology Newsgroups

sci.psychology
sci.psychology.consciousness
sci.psychology.journals.psyche
sci.psychology.misc
sci.psychology.personality
sci.psychology.psychotherapy
sci.psychology.research
sci.psychology.theory
alt.psychology.personality
alt.angst
alt.psychology.behavior.internet
alt.psychology.help
alt.psychology.jung
alt.psychology.nlp
alt.psychology.synchronicity
alt.psychology.transpersonal

Appendix II
Documenting Your Electronic Sources

Copyright laws came into effect when people started realizing that income could be made by selling their words. In an era dubbed "The Age of Information," knowledge and words are taking on more significance than ever. Laws requiring writers to *document* or give credit to the sources of their information, while evolving, are still in effect.

Various organizations have developed style manuals detailing, among other style matters, how to document sources in their particular disciplines. For writing in English composition and literature, Modern Language Association (MLA) and American Psychological Assocation (APA) guidelines are the most commonly used, but others such as those in *The Chicago Manual of Style* (CMS), are available. Always find out from your instructor what style to use in a specific assignment so that you can follow the appropriate guidelines.

For general information on MLA and APA citations, the best print sources are:

Gibaldi, Joseph. <u>MLA Handbook for Writers of Research Papers</u>. 4th ed. NY: MLA, 1995.

American Psychological Association. <u>Publication Manual of the American Psychological Association</u>. 4th ed. Washington: APA, 1994.

Because the methods of obtaining electronic information are developing so rapidly, printed style manuals have had difficulty in keeping up with the changes and in developing documentation styles for electronic sources. As a result, the most up-to-date information from the MLA and the APA about documenting online sources with URLs can be found on these organizations' Web sites. This Appendix shows you how to credit your electronic sources based on the information there.

When you cite electronic sources, it is vital to type every letter, number, symbol, and space accurately. Any error makes it impossible to retrieve your source. Since electronic sources tend to be transitory, printing a hard copy of your sources will make it easier for you to cite accurately and provide evidence for your documentation. MLA style encloses Internet addresses and URLs (Uniform Resource Locators) in angle brackets < >. If you see them around an address, do not use them as part of the address when you attempt to retrieve the source. APA style does not enclose URLs.

Modern Language Association (MLA) Style Guidelines

These guidelines follow the documentation style authorized by the Modern Language Association for electronic sources. Web sources are documented in basically the same way as traditional sources. According to the MLA Web site, the following items should be included if they are available:

1. Name of the author, editor, compiler, or translator of the source (if available and relevant), reversed for alphabetizing and followed by an abbreviation, such as *ed.*, if appropriate
2. Title of a poem, short story, article, or similar short work within a scholarly project, database, or periodical (in quotation marks); or title of a posting to a discussion list or forum (taken from the subject line and put in quotation marks), followed by the description *Online posting*
3. Title of a book (underlined)

4. Name of the editor, compiler, or translator of the text (if relevant and if not cited earlier), preceded by the appropriate abbreviation, such as *ed.*
5. Publication information for any print version of the source
6. Title of the scholarly project, database, periodical, or professional or personal site (underlined); or, for a professional or personal site with no title, a description such as *Home page*
7. Name of the editor of the scholarly project or database (if available)
8. Version number of the source (if not part of the title) or, for a journal, the volume number, issue number, or other identifying number
9. Date of electronic publication, of the latest update, or of posting
10. For a posting to a discussion list or forum, the name of the list or forum
11. The number range or total number of pages, paragraphs, or other sections, if they are numbered
12. Name of any institution or organization sponsoring or associated with the Web site
13. Date when the researcher accessed the source
14. Electronic address, or URL, of the source (in angle brackets)

From the Modern Language Association (MLA) <http://www.mla.org/main.stl.htm>.

Examples:

Book

Shaw, Bernard. Pygmalion. 1912. Bartleby Archive. 6 Mar. 1998 <http://www.columbia.edu/acis/bartleby/shaw/>.

Poem

Carroll, Lewis. "Jabberwocky." 1872. 6 Mar. 1998. <http://www.jabberwocky.com/carroll/jabber/jabberwocky.html>.

Article in a Journal

Rehberger, Dean. "The Censoring of Project #17: Hypertext Bodies and Censorship." Kairos 2.2 (Fall 1997): 14 secs. 6 Mar. 1998 <http://english.ttu.edu/kairos/2.2/index_f.html>.

Article in a Magazine

Viagas, Robert, and David Lefkowitz. "Capeman Closing Mar. 28." Playbill 5 Mar. 1998. 6 Mar. 1998 <http://www1.playbill.com/cgi-bin/plb/news?cmd=show&code=30763>.

Posting to a Discussion List

Grumman, Bob. "Shakespeare's Literacy." Online posting. 6 Mar. 1998. Deja News. <humanities.lit.author>.

Scholarly Project

Voice of the Shuttle: Web Page for Humanities Research. Ed. Alan Liu. Mar. 1998. U of California Santa Barbara. 8 Mar. 1998 <http://humanitas.ucsb.edu/>.

Professional Site

The Nobel Foundation Official Website. The Nobel Foundation. 28 Feb. 1998 <http://www.nobel.se/>.

Personal Site

Thiroux, Emily. Home page. 7 Mar. 1998 <http://academic.csubak.edu/home/acadpro/departments/english/engthrx.htmlx>.

Synchronous Communications (such as MOOs, MUDs, and IRCs)

Ghostly Presence. Group Discussion. telnet 16 Mar. 1997 <moo.du.org:8000/80anon/anonview/1 4036#focus>.

Gopher Sites

```
Banks, Vickie, and Joe Byers. "EDTECH." 18 Mar. 1997 <gopher://ericyr.syr.edu:70/00/Listservs
    /EDTECH/README>.
```

FTP (File Transfer Protocol) Sites

```
U.S. Supreme Court directory. 6 Mar. 1998 <ftp://ftp.cwru.edu/U.S.Supreme.Court/>.
```

American Psychological Association (APA) Style Guidelines

The most recent (4th) edition of the *Publication Manual of the American Psychological Association* includes general guidelines for citing electronic sources, and the APA has published specific examples for documenting Web sources on its Web page. Go to:

http://www.apa.org/journals/webref.html

In general, document these source as you do traditional sources, giving credit to the author and including the title and date of publication. Include as much information as possible to help your reader to be able to retrieve the information. Any sources that are not generally available to your readers should be documented within the body of your writing as a personal communication but not included in your reference list. Such sources include material from listservs, newsgroups, Internet relay chats (IRCs), MOOs, MUDs, and e-mail.

According to information at the Web site for the American Psychological Association entitled "How to Cite Information From the World Wide Web"*

All references begin with the same information that would be provided for a printed source (or as much of that information as possible). The Web information is then placed at the end of the reference. It is important to use the "Retrieved from" and the date because documents on the Web may change in content, move, or be removed from a site altogether. . . . To cite a Web site in text (but not a specific document), it's sufficient to give the address (e.g., http://www.apa.org) there. No reference entry is needed.

*http://www.apa.org/journals/webref.html

Use the following guidelines to include a source in your reference list:

```
Name of author [if given]. (Publication date) [in parentheses]. Title of the article [fol-
lowing APA guidelines for capitalization]. Title of periodical or electronic text [underlined].
Volume number and/or pages [if any]. Retrieved [include the date here] from the World Wide Web:
[include the URL here, and do not end with a period]
```

Examples:

Journal Article

```
    Fine, M. A. & Kurdek, L. A. (1993, November). Reflections on determining authorship
credit and authorship order on faculty-student collaborations. American Psychologist, 48.11,
1141-1147. Retrieved March 6, 1998 from the World Wide Web:
http://www.apa.org/journals/amp/kurdek.html
```

Newspaper Article

```
    Murray, B. (1998, February). Email bonding with your students. APA Monitor [Newspaper,
selected stories on line]. Retrieved March 6, 1998 from the World Wide Web:
http://www.apa.org/monitor/bond.html
```

Appendix III
Evaluating Online Sources
Look Before You Link—URLs

The books and periodicals that you access in a college library are organized and screened for reliability by librarians. But what if you are looking for information on the World Wide Web? The Web is a great place to find information, but the information is not organized, and the sources of information are not always credible or useful. Anyone with a little server space can put out information or misinformation. It is essential, then, to learn how to access and screen materials you find on the Web to ensure that you are, in fact, accessing accurate data.

How do you discern reliable and unreliable sources on the Internet? And more specifically, how do you know which sources would be best to use in a research paper or essay? Before you visit a site, there are some ways of evaluating its usefulness for your purpose. As you peruse the links listed on your search results page, try to eliminate sites *before* you visit them.

First, you should be very clear as to your teacher's instructions regarding acceptable and unacceptable sources. If your instructor is familiar with the Web, then she will probably have some guidelines for you to follow. For example, she might stipulate that for this project you may not use personal home pages or that you may not use sites sponsored by advocacy organizations, although perhaps those sources would be valid for a different kind of project. Second, you will need to have a clear focus of the nature of your project, for that will determine the types of sources that you will use.

Although not a sure-fire way to check the validity of a source, a trick to help you sift through the results page of a Web query is to check the URL (Uniform Resource Locator) for information about the site's source. Each URL has a couple of basic parts just like a residential address. Think of it as a postal address strung together without any spaces. The three main components of a URL are the **protocol**, the **domain**, and the **path**. Sometimes the **file type** is indicated as well.

The protocol of the URL indicates how the information is stored. The most common protocol you will be working with in a Web search is **http** (hypertext transfer protocol), but you might also encounter **gopher** (a menu file retrieval service), **telnet** (to log on to a remote computer) and **ftp** (file transfer protocol) sources as well. Not too long ago, you would have needed a separate program to access gopher, ftp, and sites with other protocols; now you can access most of them with your Web browser.

The domain indicates the organization, and the domain suffix indicates the type of organization. In the near future, domain names will probably expand and change to accommodate increased Web size. For now, the most common domain endings are *.gov, .com, .org, .net,* and *.edu.* Domain names that end in *.gov* are government sites; *.org* sites are nonprofit organizations; *.com* and *.net* usually indicate commercial sites or sites that support personal home pages; *.edu* indicates educational sites. You can tell a lot about a site before you visit it, then, just by looking at the domain.

Don't just trust or mistrust a site, though, because it has a particular domain name. Just because a URL has *.edu* in it doesn't necessarily make it a valid research source. You might find student hypertext projects or student home pages that might provide you with helpful links to scholarly or credible sources, but you won't want to use a student home page as a source in your research paper. On the other hand, don't mistrust a *.com* site just because it is commercial. Look at the domain for this address, for example. Many commercial sites are devoted to communicating pertinent and important information to the public. But looking before you link is a good way to avoid frustration as you search for information.

The path indicates the location of the Web page on the server. It is possible that the file name and type will be indicated as well. To put it all together, examine the following URL:

http://www.blinncol.edu/disted/tips.html

HTTP indicates the language (hypertext), blinncol.edu is the domain name (an educational site), the path or part of the server that hosts the file is disted, and the file name is tips. The .html extension indicates that this file is a Web page.

Glossary
Fasten Your Seatbelts
Jargon to Go

And a technological extension of our bodies designed to alleviate physical stress can bring on psychic stress that may be much worse.

ActiveX   This is a resource developed by Microsoft to extend the function of their *Internet Explorer* software.

Archie   This is a search tool used to find resources that are stored on Internet-based FTP servers. Archie is short for Archive because it performs an archive search for resources. (See *FTP* and *Server.*)

AVI   This stands for Audio/Video Interleaved. It is a Microsoft Corporation format for encoding video and audio for digital transmission.

Background   This refers to an image or color that is present in the background of a viewed Web document. Complex images are becoming very popular as backgrounds but require a great deal more time to download. The color of the default background can be set for most Web browsers.

Bookmark   This refers to a list of URLs saved within a browser. The user can edit and modify the bookmark list to add and delete URLs as the user's interests change. *Bookmark* is a term used by Netscape to refer to the user's list of URLs; *Hotlist* is used in *Mosaic* for the same purpose. (See *Hotlist, Mosaic,* and *URL.*)

Browser   This is a software program that is used to view and browse information on the Internet. Browsers are also referred to as clients. (See *Client.*)

Bulletin Board Service   This is an electronic bulletin board. It is sometimes referred to as a BBS. Information on a BBS is posted to a computer where people can access, read, and comment on it. A BBS may or may not be connected to the Internet. Some are accessible by modem dial-in only.

Cache   This refers to a section of memory that is set aside to store information that is frequently used by the computer . Most browsers will create a cache for commonly accessed images. An example might be the images appearing in the user's homepage. Retrieving images from the cache is much quicker than downloading the images from the original source each time they are required.

Chat room   This is a site that allows real-time, person-to-person interactions.

Clickable image (Clickable map)   This refers to an interface used in Web documents that allow the user to click, or select, different areas of an image and receive different responses. Clickable images are becoming a popular way to offer a user many different selections within a common visual format.

Client   This is a software program used to view information from remote computers. Clients function in a Client-Server information exchange model. This term may also be loosely applied to the computer that is used to request information from the server. (See *Server*.)

Compressed file   This refers to a file or document that has been compacted to save memory space so that it can be easily and quickly transferred through the Internet.

Download   This is the process of transferring a file, document, or program from a remote computer to a local computer. (See *Upload*.)

E-mail   This is the short name for electronic mail. E-mail is sent electronically from one person to one or many other people. Some companies have e-mail systems that are not part of the Internet.

FAQ   This stands for Frequently Asked Questions. A FAQ is a file or document in which a moderator or administrator will post commonly asked questions and their answers. If you have a question, you should check for the answer in a FAQ first.

Forms   This refers to an interface element used within Web documents to allow the user to send information back to a Web server. With a forms interface, the user is requested to type responses within entry windows to be returned to the server for processing. Forms rely on a server computer to process the submittals. They are becoming more common as browser and server software improve.

FTP   This stands for *File Transfer Protocol*. It is a procedure used to transfer large files and programs from one computer to another. Access to the computer to transfer files may or may not require a password. Some FTP servers are set up to allow public access by anonymous log-on. This process is referred to as *Anonymous FTP*.

GIF   This stands for Graphics Interchange Format. It is a format created by CompuServe to allow electronic transfer of digital images. GIF files are a commonly-used format and can be viewed by both *Macintosh* and *Windows* users.

Gopher   This is a format structure and resource for providing information on the Internet. It was created at the University of Minnesota

GUI   This is an acronym for Graphical User Interface. It is a combination of the appearance and the method of interacting with a computer. A GUI requires the use of a mouse to select commands on an icon-based monitor. *Macintosh* and *Windows* operating systems use GUIs.

Helper   This is software that is used to help a browser view information formats that it couldn't normally view.

Homepage This refers to a Web document that a browser loads as a point of departure to browse the Internet. It also refers to a Web page maintained by an individual. In the most general sense, it is used to refer to any Web document.

Hotlist This is a list of URLs saved within the *Mosaic* Web browser. This same list is referred to as a *Bookmark* within the Netscape Web browser.

HTML An abbreviation for HyperText Markup Language, the common language used to write documents that appear on the World Wide Web.

HTTP An abbreviation for HyperText Transport Protocol, the common protocol used to communicate between World Wide Web servers.

Hypertext This refers to text elements within a document that have an embedded connection to another item. Web documents use hypertext links to access documents, images, sounds, and video files from the Internet.

Inline image This refers to images that are viewed along with text on Web documents. All inline images are in the GIF format. JPEG format is the other common image format for Web documents; an external viewer is typically required to view JPEG documents.

Java This is an object-oriented programming language developed by Sun Microsystems.

JavaScript This is a scripting language developed by Netscape in cooperation with Sun Microsystems to add functionality to the basic Web page. It is not as powerful as *Java* and works primarily from the client side.

JPEG This stands for Joint Photographic Experts Group. It is also commonly used to refer to a format used to transfer digital images. (See *Inline image*.)

Jughead This is a service for performing searches on the Internet. (See *Archie* and *VERONICA*.)

Mosaic This is the name of the browser that was created at the National Center for Supercomputing Applications. It was the first Web browser to have a consistent interface for the Macintosh, Windows, and UNIX environments. The success of this browser is responsible for the expansion of the Web.

MPEG This stands for Motion Picture Experts Group. It is also a format used to make, view, and transfer both digital audio and digital video files.

Newsgroup This is the name for the discussion groups that can be on the *Usenet*. Not all newsgroups are accessible through the Internet. Some are accessible only through a modem connection. (See *Usenet*.)

Plug-in This is a resource that is added to the Netscape *Navigator* to extend its basic function.

QuickTime   This is a format used by Apple Computer to make, view, edit, and send digital audio and video.

Server   This is a software program used to provide or serve information to remote computers. Servers function in a Client-Server information exchange model. This term may also be loosely applied to the computer that is used to serve the information. (See *Client.*)

Table   This refers to a specific formatting element found in HTML pages. Tables are used on HTML documents to visually organize information.

Telnet   This is the process of remotely connecting and using a computer at a distant location.

Upload   This is the process of moving or transferring a document, file, or program from one computer to another computer.

URL   This is an abbreviation for Universal Resource Locator. It is an address used by people on the Internet to locate documents. URLs specify the protocol for information transfer, the host computer address, the path to the desired file, and the name of the file requested.

Usenet   This is a world-wide system of discussion groups, also called newsgroups. There are many thousands of newsgroups, but only a percentage of these are accessible from the Internet.

VERONICA   This stands for *Very Easy Rodent-Oriented Netwide Index to Computerized Archives*. This is a database of menu names from a large number of Gopher servers. It is a quick and easy way to search Gopher resources for information by keyword. It was developed at the University of Nevada.

VRML   This stands for Virtual Reality Markup Language. It was developed to allow the creation of virtual reality worlds. Your browser may need a specific plug-in to view VRML pages.

WAIS   This stands for Wide Area Information Servers. This is a software package that allows the searching of large indices of information on the Internet.

WAV   This stands for Waveform sound format. It is a Microsoft Corporation format for encoding sound files.

Web (WWW)   This stands for the World Wide Web. When loosely applied, this term refers to the Internet and all of its associated elements, including Gopher, FTP, HTTP, and others. More specifically, this term refers to a subset of the servers on the Internet that use HTTP to transfer hyperlinked document in a page-like format.